"Steve Darter's book draws you from one page and story to the next. I found the writing to be magnetic, sentence after sentence. The communication is clear and deep; nothing hidden, so painfully honest. The message about life and purpose, consistent and growing, illustrated through struggles, victories, and defeats that are so real."

—**Arthur F. Miller, author of** *The Power of Uniqueness,* *The Truth About You, Look No Further, How God Shapes Our Lives,* **and other books; founder of SIMA International**

Also by Steven M. Darter

Managing Yourself, Managing Others: Learn How to Improve Effectiveness, Productivity, and Work Satisfaction

LESSONS FROM LIFE

FOUR KEYS to Living with More Meaning, Purpose, and Success

STEVEN M. DARTER

The poem "If" by Rudyard Kipling reprinted by permission of the Rights Manager, National Trust.

All inquiries should be addressed to Steven M. Darter, www.StevenDarter.com or www.PeopleManagementSMD.com

Acknowledgments to the editor, Libbye Morris, and the graphic designer, Carol Ingaro, for the cover design.

ISBN-13: 978-1981970919

To my father, a great storyteller

"The purposes of a person's heart are deep waters,

but one who has insight draws them out"

(Proverbs 20:5)

TABLE OF CONTENTS

INTRODUCTORY COMMENTS

"The course of my life changed forever after I discovered my Motivated Abilities Pattern® with the help of Steve Darter and his associates. When JRR Tolkien wrote *The Lord of the Rings*, he thought he was writing it just for his own kids. Likewise, Steve thought he was writing just for his kids, but this deeply personal exploration of how he came to understand his design and what he discovered about applying it throughout his life in his family, career, and spiritual journey make it a useful guide packed with insights for all of us who want to live life to the fullest! This book reveals an amazing, intelligent, and proven way to discover your life's purpose."
—**Dick Staub, nationally syndicated broadcaster and founder of *The Kindlings*; author of *About You: Fully Human Fully Alive, The Culturally Savvy Christian,* and other books**

"This honest story of your life's journey is such a powerful way for you to help us all reflect on and better understand our own journeys in such a constructive frame of reference. Having had the pleasure of knowing you, watching you MAP® and positively impact the lives of hundreds of our highest-potential people, and being so influenced by you in my own life, the sharing of your life's journey is a powerful and inspiring experience. I found myself laughing at times and shedding tears of emotion at others. I literally couldn't put your book down after I started it. It was like holding up a mirror for me to think about my own life's journey and how many similar struggles I have shared with you. How powerful self-reflection can be, and as with so many other things in life, it gives me comfort to know I'm not alone as I reflect on the good, the bad, and the ugly. Everyone who reads this will benefit from its honest self-reflection and will be inspired to find the hidden strength their life journey has to make them better people."
—**Kenneth Klepper, Cofounder, Chairman, and CEO, ReactiveCore; former president and COO, Medco Health Solutions, Inc.; business board director, U.S. Department of Defense; and board of directors, U.S. Naval Institute**

"Steve Darter exhibits extreme courage, humility, and vulnerability as he tells a fascinating story of his lifelong journey leading to self-discovery of his God-given giftedness and life purpose. All readers will relate to many of Steve's experiences that are often humorous, inspiring, and emotional. But the value of this book goes well beyond the impact of interesting memoirs. In it, through provocative questions for reflection, he encourages readers to understand their own giftedness and life purpose and thereby the drivers of future happiness and personal fulfillment. This book can significantly enhance your life!"

—**Fred Sievert, retired president, New York Life Insurance Company; author of** *God Revealed: Revisit Your Past to Enrich Your Future* **and** *Grace Revealed: Finding God's Strength in Any Crisis*

"Steve Darter describes, in a compelling manner, his life's work in pursuing the identification of what it takes to have a best chance of finding a rewarding, meaningful, and successful career and life. Using expertly told stories from his own experiences as a business consultant and mentor to many different individuals, he presents our dual challenge: to determine those talents we are motivated to pursue and to find the roles to play in society, using that skill set, that is most rewarding. I met Steve in the late '80s and began working with him to find better direction for my career and my work as a CEO. Applying the motivated abilities analysis approach to my work and exposing other senior management to it was highly rewarding to the team. I have used the principles in subsequent positions successfully and wish I had been exposed to them in earlier jobs. Steve discusses all the features of this fascinating approach: defining your strengths and managing them, how God enters the picture, implementing findings in a rational and loving manner, and learning from challenges and successes. I highly recommend Steve's book for everyone desiring to use their God-given gifts to their fullest in a more fulfilling role in their professions—and in life."

—**Stephen D. Ban, PhD, former president and CEO, Gas Research Institute; retired member, board of directors, UGI Corp, Energen, and Amerigas**

"*Lessons from Life* seeks to tackle life's biggest questions—questions of meaning, purpose, and truth. Given his background, Steve Darter is uniquely positioned to explore such heady topics, and he does so marvelously in *Lessons from Life*. Throughout the book, Steve distills incredible wisdom from his own life's experiences—a life that cannot be described as anything less than a grand and wild adventure. Written with wit, humility, and heart, the stories Steve tells convey immense emotional strength. I often felt in myself the very emotions that Steve must have experienced in his stories—frequently laughing one moment, only to be startled by a moment of great poignancy the next. *Lessons from Life* truly conveys the full spectrum of human experience. Steve incisively mines his life's experience to come to a deep understanding of his own meaning, purpose, and truth, and simultaneously equips us to do the same. I definitely enjoyed learning about Steve through the book, but more importantly, I learned a lot about myself."

—Greg Baumer, senior vice president and chief growth officer, naviHealth; author (with John Cortines) of *God and Money: How We Discovered True Riches at Harvard Business School*

"In *Lessons from Life*, Steve Darter distills years of wisdom and experience into a compelling and concise narrative, as engaging as it is inspirational. The questions at the end of each chapter help readers connect their own lives and goals directly to the lessons Steve has gathered from his own vast experience. After working with Steve and identifying my Motivated Abilities Pattern®, I expected to find myself at a professional crossroads. What surprised me was discovering that I was at a spiritual turning point. After completing our work together, I reconnected with my core values and invited God back into my life. Our gifts and talents are just that— blessings from God that, when fully identified and nurtured, can focus our energies and magnetically pull goodness and success into our lives. *Lessons from Life* leads the reader directly and clearly to the center of life's purpose. Truly a life-changing book!"

—Robert Rex Waller, Jr., Associate Professor of Writing, University of Southern California; co-song writer and lead singer for the critically acclaimed roots band "I See Hawks in L.A."

"The Big Question facing all of us has to be what is the purpose of my life? Why am I here? Steve Darter dives deeply into this question in his new book *Lessons from Life* for the benefit of all who search for insight, direction, and answers. Drawing on his many years of professional experience guiding others to find meaning in their working environment and on his belief in God, Steve gently provides the outline, palette, contours, and framework of an image of 'the purpose of a life' that resonates deeply and, upon reflection, results in a compelling basis for the reader to complete the picture for his or her own life. His words, examples, and message are clear, simple, and to the point: come to know and embrace your God-given design, and let that be the foundation for all you do, experience, and give to others as you evolve on your journey."

—David T. Emott, retired CFO, Ensign-Bickford Industries; author of *Practitioner's Complete Guide to M&As*

"In this thoughtful and deeply personal book, Steve Darter addresses one of the most important and central questions in life: How can one find more purpose and meaning in his or her life? While there are many ways to answer this question, in *Lessons from Life* Steve makes the case that one path is to boldly engage in a journey of personal discovery and development. For him, this journey began by first recognizing we all have God-given talents and gifts that, when managed well, can lead to joy, but when mismanaged can lead to disappointment. Armed with this insight, he subsequently discovered that to make full and proper use of these talents, it is critical to let God into your life, to express your goodness in every day acts, and to understand that life will become more meaningful once you accept that difficulties and challenges are an essential part of clarifying what your true purpose is in life. Much more than an engaging autobiography, this thought-provoking book is a call for reflection and action. I highly recommend it for anyone who ever has or currently is seeking to find more purpose and meaning in his or her life."

—James W. Fairfield-Sonn, PhD, Professor of Management, Former Dean of the Barney School of Business, University of Hartford and Author of *Corporate Culture and the Quality Organization*

"Steve probes deep into understanding what makes us more complete as people. Using himself as a real-life example, through marvelous storytelling he effectively summarizes and develops four key aspects that have led him to be more in alignment with his life's purpose and to experience joyful, positive emotions along the way. Intriguing, courageous, and thought-provoking, *Lessons from Life* caused me to take an inventory of my personal situation and is encouraging further exploration and alignment with my life's purpose."
—**Frank Pacholec, PhD, VP Strategy and Corporate Development, Stepan Company**

"Steve's engaging life stories—each with important lessons for all—point to the imperative of finding one's unique design and purpose to be fulfilled. He shares years of experience of giving people their Motivated Abilities Pattern® through a powerful process of discovery that benefited me so many years ago! I agree with him that each of us has a unique, God-designed purpose that is discoverable. This book will move you in that direction."
—**Robert C. Andringa, PhD, President Emeritus, Council for Christian Colleges & Universities**

"Coupled with wisdom garnered from guiding others to leverage their true giftedness, Steve offers us the powerful reflections that have emerged from his own life story. The chapter exercises guide us to face the mysteries, storms, fears, and risks of personal change and to unpack and celebrate that which comes to us naturally and easily. Steve shows us how to acknowledge joy in the journey of doing what we were designed to do and *being* who we are meant to *be*. This is a book you will read, reread, and gift to others."
—**Zara F. Larsen, Executive Vice President and Global Head of Engineering, Werner International POC GmbH; former president, The Larsen Group and live talk radio show host**

"With the wisdom of the years, Steve Darter presents a sincere reflection on life's journey. Learning to appreciate and manage his own giftedness, Steve shares insights with illustrations from his own life. He offers reflection questions for the reader to ponder. Because we all yearn to live a meaningful, purposeful life, there is something for everyone in this book."
—**Margaret Crowley, RSM, PhD, a Sister of Mercy; founder of several education and health care organizations and, most recently, developing programs in workplace spirituality**

"Steve's writings embrace a common thread of longing that we all share—that is, to simply be where (and who) we are meant to be. His stories share the ebb and flow of being human while the 'gift of purpose' is revealed. The framework of belief that we are made with specific gifts and talents takes real and living form as we walk with Steve through moments of discovery. Clearly Steve's journey is ongoing, as all are, and his book reminds and heartens patience within our own and one another's path. For those who have found learning in school difficult and frustrating, Steve's experience and insights should be very helpful."
—**Edward Bouquillon, PhD, superintendent of the Minuteman Regional Vocational Technical School District**

"Whether you are early or late in your life journey, there is much to learn or relearn from Steve Darter's *Lessons from Life*. When I had an unplanned exit after thirty years as a senior executive for a major insurer, Steve showed me my Motivated Abilities Pattern®, which convinced me to radically change my career. What a great run—a new challenge almost every day, friendships with countless new people, and unexpected financial success! Steve describes many lessons he has learned that have helped him live a productive life. His book has convinced me to write my own life experience to share with my children and grandchildren. I encourage others to do the same!"
—**Sam Havens, retired president, Prudential Health Care; former chair of the board, American Health Insurance Plans; and currently a solo entrepreneur working as a board member and advisor to early-stage health services companies**

"Have you ever stopped and taken the time to thoughtfully consider what makes you special—that is, your unique gifts and natural, God-given abilities? Well, here's your chance. Steve Darter helps us explore and identify our life's purpose by sharing his own personal story. He courageously shares his successes, failures, and experiences with thought-provoking questions at the end of each chapter. Join Steve on this personal journey of reflection and growth and, like me, get a deeper, more meaningful appreciation and understanding of your life's purpose."
—Ed Landry, founder and leader, Jobs Assistance Ministry

How This Book Began and Took Shape

In 2002, after moving my parents into a nursing home, I found a diary my mother had written when she was seventeen years old, when she met my father. It felt both odd and compelling to read what she was experiencing as a teenager who was just starting to grow into womanhood and what she felt and thought, particularly about this man she just met—my father. I also found poems and stories my father wrote to my mother, about her— his newfound love—and the tragedies he had already experienced in his young life, and poems she wrote to him. I was in awe. To get that deep into the minds of my parents was quite an emotional experience.

I thought about the power and impact reading their words had on me, particularly as their lives here on Earth were coming to an end. I decided that I wanted to provide my kids the same feeling—the same sense of awareness, awe, impact, and emotionalism. My intent was to write some stories about my life that they might find upon my death.

I know that may sound a bit weird, but just as I had a wonderful reaction to reading what my parents wrote, I thought that my kids, and perhaps my grandkids, might find reading what I wrote a wonderful experience. That is how this book began. But along the way, the nature of the book took a turn. The stories became my way of looking at my life and grappling with questions about meaning, purpose, and success, which led to the larger question: "What is the purpose of my life?"

When I had spare time to write these stories, which I had little of, I would do so very early in the morning, when all was quiet. I would lie in bed, in the dark, and let my mind wander until it settled on a memory. Then I would get up, make myself a cup of tea, and take a journey into my mind. I had no outline or idea where a story would lead me, but lead me each story did.

Early in the process, when I was thinking that I was just writing something for my kids to read after I died, I had lunch with Art Miller, a mentor, friend, and former boss who knows me well.

"It will not be enough; you will need to write something you can share with many people, something that would have a positive impact and influence on many lives," he said.

"You're wrong. Writing something just for my kids, and perhaps my grandkids, will be enough," I replied.

But as I began sharing the stories I had written with others, I realized that Art was right.

I hope my book opens your mind, touches your heart, connects with your spirit, brings you smiles and tears, and inspires you to think about the purpose of your life and your life journey—and to appreciate its profoundness.

A Note from Steve Darter

Have you ever wondered what the purpose of *your* life is? What the secret is to living a life that has meaning? What path *you* should take to achieve *your* purpose? Do you even believe you have a purpose? How about an intended destiny?

Most, if not all of us, have asked (or will ask) ourselves these types of questions at some point in our lives—even if it is only at the end. For me, these questions were like a rhythmic wave that kept returning—something I needed an answer to—something I couldn't let go of. So I delved deeply.

In 1975, long before these questions took up residence within me, I began what has turned out to be a highly successful forty-plus-year career that involved evaluating and advising people—ranging from troubled teenagers to CEOs of Fortune 500 corporations—on work, career, and life issues. I calculate that I have interviewed close to five thousand people during those forty-plus years.

In each interview, I was trying to understand the person's unique natural talent and best path for success and, in some cases, what had gotten in their way. This vantage point gave me an unusually close-up view of how people's lives unfolded, including their successes and failures, the impact of decisions they made, actions they took, beliefs they adopted, course corrections they attempted, regrets, feelings of disappointment and failure, and satisfaction.

As I interviewed people, I often felt as if I were inside them—inside their hearts and souls. Many of the conversations were quite deep, meaningful, and revealing. I often felt as if I were sitting at the edge of a universe, making observations—discovering. And despite what a person may have felt about him or herself, I was in awe of the people I met and interviewed. There was something quite unique and special about each person.

The glimpses I had into the lives of others caused me to reflect on my life continually. Along the way, from all those interviews, conversations, observations, and reflections, I began learning what makes a life purposeful and meaningful. This dramatically affected me—not in one quick, magical moment, but slowly over time as I changed from the inside out and from the outside in.

I learned that there was a lot of garbage hanging on me, hanging on my branches, that needed to be cleaned off—garbage that blocked the light, stunting my progress and growth. As I cleaned off the garbage and let the sun shine on my branches, I realized that I was becoming (or perhaps returning to) who I was designed to be.

Through the initial haze, and later with greater clarity, I could see that the more I was in sync with my design, the more I had the feeling that I was living my life with meaning and purpose. And the more I was living my life with meaning and purpose, the closer I was coming to fulfilling my intended destiny.

The Four Keys

I came to believe that there are four important key aspects that make up my design. What is true for me, I believe is also true for you. The following four keys are the basis of this book:

1. **You have been designed with giftedness** It is important to understand your unique giftedness—your natural talent—and to manage it well. Doing so can be an incredible asset, strength, and source of purpose and fulfillment. If it is not understood and managed well, it can lead to a disappointing life and perhaps failure. Section 1 illustrates the value of understanding and managing *your* giftedness—*your* natural talent—and provides exercises to help you understand and manage this unique key aspect of your design.

2. **You have been designed to seek a relationship with (and experience) God.** People all over the world, regardless of location and culture, seek God. It seems to be embedded within all of us. Doing so will fill a hole—an emptiness that many of us have tried to fill with other things. Regardless of how long it takes and what you need to experience, it is important to eventually allow God to be in your life—even if you are at the end of a long road—and to allow His presence to grow within you, on an emotional level as well as an intellectual one. For me to write this feels quite

remarkable. In section 2, I explain how I came to this understanding and provide some pointed questions for you to consider, as you evaluate the relevance of this key aspect of your design.

3. **You have been designed to express love and goodness.** There is much benefit in being compassionate; doing what is good and right; controlling envy, anger, arrogance, and resentment; and expressing love, kindness, generosity, and appreciation. Doing so will bring out and reinforce the best that has been placed inside you, enabling you to live with more meaning and purpose. Section 3 illustrates this concept and key aspect of your design and includes questions to help you examine how such behaviors and beliefs have impacted (and can potentially impact) your life.

4. **You have been designed to learn from difficulties and challenges.** This doesn't mean we don't learn, grow, and develop from positive experiences, but difficulties and challenges (and we all have them) can propel you forward, producing incredible growth within you, if you allow it. Section 4 illustrates how such moments can become springboards and also includes questions to ask yourself as you consider the power this key aspect of your design has to change your life.

If these four key aspects of your design are understood and managed well, you will have more meaning, purpose, and success in your life and you will come closer to fulfilling your intended destiny. If any of these four key aspects of your design are buried or ignored, it will likely result in your feeling that your life could have been and should have been more—that something was missing.

Embrace Your Design

After forty-plus years of consulting, counseling, observing, reflecting, and learning, I have come to several fundamental beliefs. Here are six of them:

1. **We naturally seek to evolve toward our design.** Like salmon swimming upstream, seeking to return to their birthplace, it is in our nature to evolve toward how we have been designed. There is

much that can interfere with the process of achieving our design, but this doesn't mean that the desire to evolve toward how we have been designed disappears.

2. **We have a choice.** Each of us is given the choice to either embrace how we have been designed or fall away from it. Actually, we're given many opportunities to embrace our design—God does not give up on any of us.

3. **Meaning and purpose are built in and achieved as we seek to live out our design.** The more you embrace and evolve toward all four key aspects of your design, the more meaningful and purposeful your life will be, and the closer you will come to fulfilling your intended destiny. Conversely, the further you move away from your design, the less meaningful and purposeful your life will become, and the greater the likelihood that you will not fulfill your intended destiny.

4. **Life is more than we sometimes recognize.** Life is more than just a chance at living, dying, and experiencing, or being happy. It's more than just "making it" by earning a lot of money or achieving fame, status, visibility, or power, or just surviving, or living in such a way that we hide or bury our design. And it is broader than a purposeful moment, task, role, or job, as we often think when saying, "This is my calling—my destiny." We all have many opportunities such as these.

5. **Life is an opportunity.** Life, I believe, is an opportunity to grow, develop, and evolve toward how we have been designed. It is an opportunity to evolve our souls—to become the people God has designed us to be. Developing that perspective has had an incredibly positive impact on me.

6. **Perfection isn't the end product.** I don't think any of us can achieve the perfection of our design. But the purpose of our lives (I believe) is to try and become, as best we can, the people God intends us to be.

What does this mean? Embedded within each of us is a unique giftedness to be developed and managed well, a desire to experience God, a desire to express love and goodness, a proclivity to learn from difficulties and challenges, and a predisposition to evolve our souls continually.

Yes, there are many obstacles, hardships, roadblocks, and temptations along the way. Overcoming them and not letting them corrupt, distort, or discourage you can be very difficult. They can throw you off course if you let them. This is true whether you have achieved a lot of "success" or find yourself on the short end of health, money, freedom, or tragedy, which may seem very unfair. God challenges each of us differently as He seeks to develop our souls.

As you read each chapter, you will see that I have chosen to illustrate what I am saying by telling stories about myself and others. I do so because I love telling stories and using them to illustrate points, just as my father did. It is in my nature—my DNA. As a result, you will get to learn a lot about me and the lessons I learned from my life.

After each story, I have added questions for reflection and discussion. Please use the questions to help determine what gives your life meaning and purpose. If, like me, you find comforting answers, you will experience an inner peacefulness. It may not be present all the time, but you will find that it is never far away—never out of reach.

Your life is a journey that leads you. The question is, to where and why?

One last item before you turn the page: If you think it is too late, that your life is almost over, that you are too old, or have strayed too far, or blown your opportunity, that is not the case. Course corrections are never too late, and grace is available to all.

God, I believe, plays the long game—He doesn't give up. He wants you to keep evolving your soul to achieve all four key aspects of your design. When you do, you will come closer to realizing the purpose of your life and fulfilling your intended destiny—and this process doesn't end until your life on Earth ends.

For Reflection and Discussion

1. Why are you reading this book? What are you hoping to get from it? What are your expectations? How will you know that your expectations have been met?

2. What criteria do you use to determine if you are living a meaningful, purposeful, and successful life?

The Importance of Home

Feeling that you are anchored, grounded, and connected to something that is positive will help give your life focus, clarity, meaning, and purpose. I didn't fully realize this until I was past age fifty, but I recognized the seeds of this truth even as a young child.

Life is a journey, as most of us know, and through the journey you can make discoveries and uncover things about yourself that will have positive, enduring value.

Such moments can come early. For me, such a moment arrived like a light, wrapped in the initial darkness of fear, when I was eight years old. It happened as I ventured out alone into the larger world for the first time, away from the comforts of the streets, trees, and faces I knew, beyond the neighborhood, past the elementary school, and across the four-lane Peninsula Boulevard with its fast-moving cars.

I had convinced my parents that I was old enough to travel to the dentist's office on my own. My father was proud, standing a bit taller as I walked out the door. My mother was worried; I could see it in her eyes and on her face.

It was one mile to the corner, where a bus stopped to pick me up. I knew the route. I had walked it before, but never alone. I rode the bus through Woodmere, Cedarhurst, and Lawrence to Far Rockaway. I arrived on time, settled into a big chair, had my teeth examined, and then headed back to the bus stop, where I waited. Buses arrived and left. I got on one.

I rode past familiar buildings toward my home, daydreaming, fantasizing, imagining, and oblivious to the fact that I was not on the right bus.

Reality jolted me upright. I looked around for some bearing as to where I was, but nothing echoed in my mind—only silence.

I did what perhaps other eight-year-olds might do in such a situation: I shrank deeper into my seat and optimistically imagined that it was all going to work out OK—that I was going to end up where I was supposed to be.

The bus made its final stop, and the doors opened. I had to exit, and I did, into a place I had never seen before. I stood motionless, a small child alone, lost. People walked about, but no one took notice of me and my plight. My stomach tightened, my breathing grew shallow, my head became lighter, and my little legs grew a bit wobbly. Cold sweat arrived.

I didn't think to ask for help, nor did I think to telephone my parents—why, I still don't know. Maybe because this was not the era of cell phones, perceived dangers at every corner, and parents who hovered. This was a world of independence and self-reliance, amplified by living in the aftershock of World War II and the shadow of the Great Depression. Maybe I just didn't have enough wherewithal to think to do so, or perhaps I subconsciously responded to the challenge the situation presented. Rather than make the telephone call that would have brought help, I purchased candy bars with the change I had in my pocket.

I began to walk, taking each step with uncertainty but hope. I walked for a long time. Darkness descended. I was alone and frightened. Nothing was familiar. At each crossroads, I had to make a decision—turn left, turn right, stay the course, turn back? I had no plan and no sense of where I was headed, but I kept walking in a direction that felt right. How symbolic.

Finally, familiarity began to replace uncertainty. As it did, the path grew clearer, and decisions became easier. My steps became lighter and crisper, my shoulders became straighter, and I held my head higher. I strutted with confidence. Anticipation and excitement filled my senses.

I arrived home well into the night. My parents were panicked, but I felt alive. They wrapped their loving arms around me. There was comfort in their embrace.

That was my first encounter I recall that was shrouded with fear of the unknown, fear that comes from being lost, fear of making the wrong choice, fear of consequences, and fear of inaction.

I recall lying in bed thinking how fearful I had become, about the power that familiarity and certainty brought, and how the thought of getting home, to where I belonged, helped me stay determined, helped me overcome and persevere through my fear. And although I did not have the frame of reference at the time, it gave my life a sense of purpose.

I have come to realize that I need a *home* that provides a visual target and a safe haven from which I can comfortably venture into the world—a *home* that feeds my innate need for focus, connection, belonging, clarity, meaning, and purpose. When I didn't have that, my journey felt like endless wandering—like a lost soul looking for its resting place.

My *home* has taken many forms: belief in God; meaningful work and activity that fit my giftedness; wholesome beliefs and values I have committed to living out; a worthy effort, cause, or mission to which I dedicate time and energy; being with people I love and respect and expressing love to them; and engaging in experiences that enable me to grow, develop, and evolve toward my design and intended destiny. Often there is a combination of these.

Life journeys can lead in many directions, both good and bad, as they often do. Paths are rarely straight, but I have come to understand that being *home* (feeling that I am where I am meant to be, being who I was designed to be, and doing what I have been designed to do) can have a powerful energizing and calming effect. I have learned that this is a critical ingredient to living a meaningful and purposeful life.

I have come to believe that it is important to determine what gives your life meaning and purpose and to use that understanding to establish a life view that you strive to achieve, realize, live out, and measure yourself against. Without such a guidepost, you might lose your way.

For Reflection and Discussion

1. What are your *homes* that provide focus, connection, belonging, clarity, meaning, and purpose?
2. How has having these *homes* been helpful to you?
3. Have you ever felt lost, not anchored or grounded, with little or nothing to provide a sense of belonging, focus, connection, clarity, meaning, and purpose? If yes, what did it feel like?
4. What criteria are you using to determine if you are living a successful life?

SECTION 1

You Have Been Designed with Giftedness

PART 1

Understand Clues to Your Giftedness

CHAPTER 1

Get into the Right Game

You may or may not have ever thought about what I am about to say, but I assure you that it is the truth: when you engage in activity that fits your natural talent, you will significantly increase your odds of living a life that has meaning and purpose.

As the following story illustrates, the seeds for uncovering your natural talent emerge early in your life, and if you pay attention to them, they will be important guideposts. And when you engage in activity (or get to a place or role) that fits your natural talent, it can change your life for the better—perhaps forever. I urge you to never forget this.

I enjoyed hanging out with my older brother, Gene, almost three years my senior. We were an interesting-looking pair. He was long and lanky, like Ichabod Crane; I was built square and close to the ground. He was quiet and studious; I was cocky and obnoxious.

I looked up to Gene, as younger brothers are prone to do, but I couldn't be like him. I couldn't do well in school as he did, and I couldn't stay focused as he did. My mind was continually wandering, my mouth often arguing and challenging, and my smile deceiving—hiding the insecurities I felt. Gene accepted me (perhaps at his young age, he even knew me), and this provided a cloud of comfort on which I grew dependent.

When I entered the fourth grade, I found myself on my own. Gene moved on to junior high school. It was like he was living in another world, and I was left alone to survive in this one. I withdrew and grew quiet.

In this new world, at school, during lunch periods, I sat on the grass watching older boys play baseball. I wanted to join but was hesitant to ask. So I sat and watched, feeling invisible.

I have come to understand that people do notice, even when we think they don't—none of us is quite as invisible as we might feel.

"Steve, would you like to play?" an older boy I didn't know asked one day, vaporizing my invisibleness—penetrating my shell.

"OK," I said.

"Grab a glove. You're playing right field."

"OK."

"You're batting last."

"OK."

Right field is the position assigned to the worst player. I didn't care. My heart was pounding. I was in the game. And being in the game was better than sitting on the sidelines, invisible, watching the game.

A fly ball was hit to right field. I easily moved under the ball and caught it. I threw the ball hard to the infield. I felt alive, in sync, where I was meant to be. When I got to bat, I hit a triple. It felt great! Then I got up to bat again and hit another triple. I ran as fast as my legs would carry me around those bases. Life felt wonderful.

The next day, when teams were chosen, I was picked early. I was moved from right field to left field and then to third base. I moved up in the batting order. Several weeks later, some other older boys I didn't know asked if I wanted to be part of their team when they ran races. "OK," I said.

The decision to accept that invitation to play in that baseball game turned my life around. It was a game changer that brought me out of my shell and gave me something I could feel confident about. But what would have happened if I wasn't naturally good in athletics? How would I have felt about myself if I didn't achieve success and feel inherent satisfaction in what I was doing? Would I have shrunk back into the shadows with failure? How long would it have taken me to step forward again?

I have come to believe that it is important to get into the game, but equally important is getting into the *right* game, one at which we are naturally gifted and can perform well—one that provides an inherent sense of joy and meaning and plays into the unique strike zone each of us possesses.

For Reflection and Discussion

1. What are you naturally gifted in? What are your natural talents?
2. Have you sought to develop and use your natural talent? If not, why not?

CHAPTER 2

Recognize What Makes You Alert, Energized, and In Sync

If you understand the kinds of situations that trigger and sustain your energy and interest, you can more effectively put yourself into situations where you will thrive. By doing so, there is a greater chance you will be in sync with your nature and improve the odds of feeling that your life has meaning and purpose.

Situations that motivate and energize you can emerge from any kind of experience—even ones that might give the outside observer pause, as you can see in the following story.

After wreaking havoc along the entire Eastern seaboard, on September 12, 1960, Hurricane Donna bombarded Long Island with record-breaking winds and rainfall. I watched with fascination, my nose pressed against various window panes in our house. Adults were worried, but I was excited. I had never felt such power and force. And when the rain and winds left, I could hardly wait to get outside and explore.

"No!" I was told emphatically.

"I'll be careful," I persisted. For each *no* and reason, I had an answer. My persistence paid off.

"Don't go into the street; stay in the yard," I was told sternly.

Water was surging down our street and around the corner. Everything I could see was flooded.

Our small ranch-style home sat on a corner lot. As I walked around our house, the ground squished with each step, tree branches were down, and ants scurried about, their homes flooded.

From my pocket I pulled several used ice cream sticks, which two days earlier I had been turning into pointy knives by scraping them on the sidewalk.

I placed some ants on one of the ice cream sticks and carefully carried them on the stick to the front side of the house, placed them into the water, and ran along watching, as their raft floated down the street, around the corner, and at the far end of our property line, down the sewer. I ran back, put more ants on another stick, and did it again—several more times, until I ran out of ice cream sticks.

I looked beyond the yard, which had become containment. Excitement, I felt, lay elsewhere.

Despite the warnings and my agreement to stay in the yard, I waded into the surging water. It was a spontaneous decision made by an athletic eleven-year old whose mind rarely considered consequences when it decided to do something opportunistic that was an outgrowth of boredom, or something my instinct told me was worth trying to do or explore.

The water immediately grabbed hold of me, forcing me to step back—the same route the ants on the ice-cream-stick rafts had taken. I braced and fought the current but continued to be pushed back. My legs tried to hold their ground, but my battle was slowly being lost. At the corner, as the surging water pushed right, my small body began to fall and submerge. I reached out and grabbed the stop-sign pole, and fighting the current, pulled myself to safety.

Once on solid ground, wet but determined, I walked through neighbors' yards, down Ibsen Street to Island Avenue, where the water was not as high and the current not as strong. Into the water I went again, down the road, around the corner, and down more roads, examining the damage. I was too young to know about the danger I was putting myself in and too oblivious to appreciate my luck in not being injured, but I was very alert, energized, and in sync with my nature and who I was designed to be.

Some of the circumstances and conditions (situations) that motivate me that are apparent in this story include an opportunity to explore and discover; a need to deal with the unknown; restlessness and the need for movement, action, or pace; obstacles to overcome; and a need to persist.

When you engage in activity that has the kinds of circumstances and conditions you find inherently motivating, you will be operating closer to your giftedness strike zone and thus closer to how you have been designed. As a result, you will increase your chance of living with meaning and purpose and for realizing your intended destiny.

The circumstances and conditions that motivate and energize you are unique to you. Perhaps you are naturally drawn to needs and causes, or to problems to solve, or to emergencies that need handling. Or maybe you like having structure or a routine to follow, or no structure. Maybe you like working alone, or as part of a team, or you like being precise and exact, or haphazard. Maybe you like to develop or create something, or to be faced with deadlines, or to gain visibility, or to establish your reputation. Some situations (circumstances and conditions) will trigger your energy and motivation, some will sustain it, and some will do both.

For Reflection and Discussion

1. What kinds of situations (circumstances and conditions) do you find highly motivating and make you feel alert, energized, and in sync with your nature?

2. Have you sought to put yourself into the kinds of situations (conditions and circumstances) that enable you to feel alert, energized, and in sync with your nature? If not, why not?

CHAPTER 3

The Power of Inherent Interests

Now that you have identified circumstances and conditions that energize you, or at least have begun the process of doing so, the next step in uncovering and understanding your natural talent—your giftedness—is to identify subject areas in which you have an inherent interest.

As the following story illustrates, we are all drawn to working with different subject matter. When you work with or through subject matter that is part of your giftedness, you will come closer to how you have been designed, and you will have a better chance of living your life with meaning and purpose.

When I was fifteen years of age, my sister, Joan, who is seventeen years older than me, wanted to save me from myself. She wanted to inspire me to be more. She convinced my parents to send me to Columbus, Ohio, to spend one week with her and my then brother-in-law. He had carved out a very successful business career and, at a young age, was president of The Fashion department store.

Like me, Joan had not performed well academically in school, but despite this, she grew to become quite educated and cultured—mainly on her own. Joan wanted to wake me up as she had done. I was too oblivious to recognize her accomplishment and to see what she was attempting to do for me. Sports, gambling, and girls were the focus of my existence.

Joan tried exposing me to worlds I cared little about, like art. She even had guests over for a dinner who were all successful professionals, and they asked me what I wanted to do with my life. She did this to expose me to another world, maybe to wake me up through embarrassment.

I found the whole attempt to *wake me up* amusing. I said things to convince the well-meaning adults that I understood the message and importance of being serious about my life, my future, and pursuing a path to success. The truth was that I was more interested in the two cute girls who lived across the street.

I was pretty much confined to hanging out with Joan and her two young daughters (my nieces), but not out of punishment—I just didn't know people my age in Columbus to party with.

Joan, her then-husband Jim, and my two nieces were fun to be with, but they all went to sleep so early. I loved the night and the excitement it could bring. Going out at night was an adventure, each journey bringing discovery—but more so, the night fed my need for an adrenaline rush.

As darkness descended, I grew increasingly restless, anxious, and bored.

Joan wasn't much for television, and the only one available was too close to her bedroom for me to sneak about and chance turning it on. Besides, TV back then had only a few channels.

There was a room at Joan's that had floor-to-ceiling bookshelves, containing loads of books demonstrating the breadth of the family's reading interests and accomplishments. I sought out its contents—my only refuge.

From left to right, up and down, I read each title. Maybe something would catch my eye, something to read to make the time go by, to make the boredom cease. I tried one book, then another, and another, and another, rarely getting past a paragraph or a page.

The *Fifty-Minute Hour* by Robert Lindner seemed to be just another book. But unlike the others, it grabbed my interest from the start. "Fifty minutes" referred to a psychiatrist's hour—spending fifty minutes with a patient and having ten minutes to dictate notes.

The book was a collection of stories about people who had psychological difficulties. I read the book cover to cover, seemingly in one sitting. I don't think I had ever read a whole book prior to that, and I know I had never been absorbed in reading like that before. Doing so calmed my restlessness.

What was it about this book and subject matter that seemed to attract me like no other, outside of sports, gambling, and girls? Why was my mind thinking about these people and their situations? Why was I thinking about what I may have asked or explored if I were the psychiatrist? Why was I thinking about people I knew and wondering what may be lurking deep inside them?

As I flew back to New York, I couldn't stop thinking about the book *The Fifty-Minute Hour*. I somehow seemed to be connected to the people, their stories, and their emotions—not to their psychotic or schizophrenic personalities, but to the subject matter itself and the world of emotions.

The visit to Joan's worked—not as she had hoped, but it opened my eyes to something new, something I could connect with, something I found inherently interesting. Neither of us realized it at the time. And neither of us realized the power that inherent interests have to overcome and transcend when discovered, unleashed, and developed.

When you work with and through subject areas that highly motivate you, under circumstances and conditions that also motivate you, you will have a greater chance of feeling that your life has meaning and purpose. Consequently, you will have a greater chance of fulfilling your intended destiny.

For Reflection and Discussion
1. In which subject areas do you have an inherent interest?
2. Have you pursued and developed your interest in these subject areas? If not, why not?

CHAPTER 4

Use Your Natural Abilities

I've heard it said that ignorance comes when we are not aware of what we are not aware of. At those times, we walk in blindness or with blinders on, not seeing, not recognizing, not learning—no growth, development, or benefit—not knowing what we have missed. We've all had such moments when we are looking but not seeing.

All around are clues to your natural talent—pay attention, look, see, realize. When you can define it, nail it, and engage in activity that makes use of your unique giftedness, there is joy that consumes and radiates, resulting in a greater chance that you will feel that your life has meaning and purpose, simply because you are in sync with this important key aspect of your design.

If you have had such moments, you know what I am talking about. If you think those moments have eluded you, you have not been listening to yourself and the evidence of your giftedness.

The previous two chapters emphasized the importance of working under conditions and circumstances that make you alert, energized, and in sync and with subject matter you are inherently interested in. The following story emphasizes this, as well as the importance of using your natural abilities and interacting with people in ways that you find highly motivating.

If you were around in 1967 and paying attention, you were witness to an emotionalism within America that was ripping and tearing the fabric of society. The Vietnam War, racism, and a questioning of the American way of life were all at the root of protests and riots that began to spring up like wildfires across the vast landscape—from Detroit to Miami and New York to San Francisco, with many places in between. You could watch the action live on television. Like a giant wave or tornado, it took over the lives of some people, pushing them with tremendous force in directions they had not seen themselves taking.

If you were around in 1967 and paying attention, you were also witness to San Francisco seemingly kicking off the emergence of hippies and the Human Be-In, which gave birth to the Summer of Love, fueled by the Beatles' album *Sgt. Pepper's Lonely Hearts Club Band*. Drug use became rampant. Hair grew long. Clothes became multicolored and expressive, reflecting a drug-induced state and the new sexual revolution.

If you were around in 1967 and paying attention, you would have witnessed troop levels in Vietnam surging to 475,000; peace protests becoming more violent; Thurgood Marshall being confirmed as the first African American on the US Supreme Court; Muhammad Ali being stripped of his heavyweight crown for refusing to serve in the army; Israel defeating Egypt, Jordan, and Syria in the six-day war; the Boston Strangler being convicted; the first successful heart transplant; the first countertop microwave; the first Super Bowl; the fire on Apollo 1 that killed astronauts Grissom, Chaffee, and White; China successfully exploding its first hydrogen bomb; the musical production *Hair*; and the movies *The Graduate, Guess Who's Coming to Dinner, In the Heat of the Night, The Dirty Dozen, Cool Hand Luke, In Cold Blood, Doctor Doolittle, Wait Until Dark, The Jungle Book, Thoroughly Modern Millie, Bonnie and Clyde,* and *Camelot*. What a year!

I was finally graduating from high school, moving on autopilot, and doing but not thinking much. Through two friends, I got a summer job running a parking lot at the VIP Beach Club in Atlantic Beach on Long Island. This small, private beach club catered to upper-middle-class and affluent families.

Two friends, Scott and Mark, had secured lucrative jobs as cabana boys at the VIP, and another friend, Jeff was a lifeguard. Each day, Mark drove Scott and me to work in his blue Firebird convertible with the top down, the sun shining, the wind blowing, our hair flapping, sunglasses protecting and camouflaging, and music blasting. We were young and cool.

We had to arrive early, before 7:30 a.m. We were often tired and bleary-eyed from whatever late-night events we had collectively and individually engaged in. For me, it was mostly gambling.

I was the only person parking cars. I was my own boss—sort of. The manager of the VIP Beach Club was Andy, who was in his mid-twenties. Andy was big, about 6'5." He had played basketball in college. His hands were huge and swallowed up mine when we shook hands after he hired me.

We cut a deal. I would keep 60 percent of the money earned from parking cars, and he would get the other 40 percent. The parking lot held about two hundred cars, if I packed them in. This meant leaving just enough room between each car so that I could squeeze through the driver's-side door when opened—stacking the cars behind each other. This meant that one or more cars often needed to be moved to get to the one I wanted.

I quickly developed a good understanding of who left early and who left late, enabling me to reposition cars to make retrieving them go more smoothly. When the sun was out, I was able to earn good money—$30 on a weekday and $75 on a weekend day—after giving Andy his 40 percent cut. When it rained, I earned nothing, and when it was cloudy, I earned very little.

I thoroughly enjoyed being my own boss, working for tips, and providing top-notch service to my customers. I got so good at providing service that when I saw people walking toward the exit of the beach club, I knew which car was theirs and where I had parked it. I would run as fast as I could to have their car up front by the entrance before they arrived. I knew people by their names, by the cars they drove, and by their children. I continually received compliments, and on weekends when the husbands were present, the tips were larger.

These were successful, affluent men who would take a large wad of bills from their pockets and give me one dollar instead of a coin or two. Some would flip through the singles, peel off a five, and hand it to me with a nod or smile. I was always honest with Andy and gave him his 40 percent split.

Here's the thing: Andy never asked me if I had a driver's license, and I never told him I didn't. I never told him that I couldn't get my driver's license until after my birthday, late in August.

I was confident in my driving abilities. I'd been secretly borrowing my Aunt Ruth's car for several years and occasionally drove my dad's delivery van. And, during the school year, I had convinced another student, Henry, to let me borrow his car during my lunch period so I could leave the school grounds for lunch. Henry and I had different lunch periods. In fairness to Henry, I neglected to tell him that I didn't have a driver's license.

One day in mid-August, a lot of families were leaving all at once, and the parking lot was jammed full, like a can of packed sardines, as the saying goes, with only inches between each car. I got in a Chevy, threw the gear into reverse, and *thud*—hit the car behind that I had neglected to move. "Shit!" I yelled. I ran back, got the other key, moved the car that was blocking the way, and saw that each had some damage. I told Andy and the car owners about the damage. Andy told them that we would have the damages repaired. I was embarrassed and scared. Andy never expressed anger to me, nor did he dock my pay. Two weeks later, I passed my driver's test and obtained my license. By then, the summer season was over, and the beach club was closed.

As the summer came to a close, Mark, Scott, Jeff, and I sat on the beach by the lifeguard stand, drinking beers and talking about the paths we wanted our lives to take. The moon was full, and the sky presented compellingly dark, jagged clouds. It was an incredible bonding moment. Mostly I listened. I had no clue about what I wanted from life. "Maybe I'll be a croupier at a casino," I was thinking but didn't say. I always enjoyed dealing cards and seeing reactions in bodies and on faces. I loved the unknown of what card would turn up and observing how people would react and what actions they would take. When I had a deck of cards in my hands and dealt the cards, I felt alive and powerful.

I would love to be able to write that I learned a lot that summer about life and myself, but I didn't. Such awareness eluded me. I didn't know what to look for or what to ask. If I did, there were signs to be seen and understood. I just didn't know how to read the signs or how to pay attention to them.

The signs would have told me that providing service to others brings out the best in me—the kind of situation that energizes and stimulates me to be dedicated, disciplined, determined and, most importantly, focused. Being unable to focus in many situations was my ongoing nemesis.

I also would have realized that I loved being my own boss, figuring out how to provide excellent service, winning people over, and soaking up positive reactions to me and the service I provided. In a large measure, the way I provided service to those families at the VIP Beach Club was the same way I provided service to corporate executives later in my life—an important key to my career satisfaction and success.

I have come to understand that our life experiences shape us tremendously. But underneath the direction our lives take, there seems to be something inside that comes naturally to all people, making each of us different and unique, providing an inherent sense of satisfaction and success. Tapping into your unique giftedness and capitalizing on it is an important factor to achieving success and satisfaction in life and work and to realizing your life's purpose.

The stories people tell about themselves have always fascinated me, particularly those recalled with great pride and emotion from their childhoods—the seemingly silly stories and proud moments. Each one becomes a window to the natural gifts, talents, and orientations a person possesses.

Just as I was finishing writing this story, I received an email from an executive who had successfully battled cancer. As a result, he was more appreciative and in tune with being alive and living his life. He appreciated the consulting I was doing that helped people understand their natural abilities and talents. He had his entire management team go through the process I use to enhance team functioning and individual performance.

What he sent was not unfamiliar to me, but it was timely. I have learned that when something is timely (coincidental), there is usually a reason, usually a message to listen for, an opportunity to grow from, a chance to evolve, or a chance to reinforce something already realized. He emailed me a Scripture of the day sent to him by a friend of his who was serving as a spiritual advisor to a presidential candidate: "We have different gifts, according to the grace given us. If a man's gift may be prophesying, let him use it in proportion to his faith. If it is serving, let him serve; if it is teaching, let him teach; if it is encouraging, let him encourage; if it is contributing to the needs of others, let him give generously; if it is leadership, let him govern diligently; if it is showing mercy, let him do so cheerfully" (Rom. 12:6–8).

If I had been aware during the summer of 1967, I would have understood that something far more fundamental was at work. But all I knew back then was that I felt good about the parking service I was providing—that I felt very alive doing that job.

When you can use abilities and interact with people in ways you find highly motivating, you will have a greater chance of feeling that your life has meaning and purpose and a greater chance of fulfilling your intended destiny. This is true particularly when you can do so in situations (under circumstances and conditions) that trigger and sustain your motivational energy and when working with and through subject areas in which you have a naturally high level of interest.

For Reflection and Discussion
1. Describe the abilities you find great satisfaction in using and the ways you enjoy interacting with and relating to people.
2. Have you purposely tried to use the abilities you find great satisfaction in using? Have you tried interacting with people in ways you enjoy? If not, why not?

CHAPTER 5

A MAP for Life

I use the following story to introduce you to a process you can use to identify the circumstances and conditions, subject matter, abilities, and ways of interacting with people that you find highly motivating, as well as the concept of central motivational themes. When you can identify these for yourself and use that knowledge to put yourself into jobs, roles, careers, and activities that make use of them, you will come closer to achieving the purpose of your life and intended destiny. You also will improve your chances for feelings of success and satisfaction.

Some people you meet profoundly affect your life, almost like some sort of destiny was involved. A moment, an opportunity. Perhaps it is fate. Instinctually you respond. Almost everyone I speak with can relate to this. For me, one of those moments came in 1976 when I met Arthur F. Miller, Jr.

Art was a speaker at a conference I was attending. He arrived late one evening with gray hair flowing, looking like a mad professor or scientist, stumbling around in search of his conference host, who was a colleague of mine. I responded by asking if I could be of assistance. We began to talk.

If you have ever met Art, you would know firsthand what happened next. I innocently asked him what he was speaking about the next day, and for the next several hours, we were engaged in a conversation about people, motivation, giftedness, and human design, the likes of which I had never heard before. Art was argumentative, stubborn, intriguing, highly passionate, and very compelling.

I decided to attend Art's presentation the next day. I watched him debate, argue, and defend his beliefs before a packed room. What he said and believed astounded me, and I was drawn to learn more.

Through an interview-based process, Art saw that each person seemed to have his or her own natural style. He came to believe that when a person doesn't work out in a job, it generally has more to do with style and issues of compatibility than it does with a lack of technical background or experience. He began to see that each person is different—unique, an individual, a snowflake, a thumbprint—and that much satisfaction and success at work is tied to using one's natural gifts and talents.

Art pursued this observation and discovered that residing within each of us is a natural pattern of motivation that triggers us to perform our best, which in turn sustains us and drives us. For each person, the pattern is different. He called this phenomenon a Motivated Abilities Pattern® (MAP®).

Art discovered the following:

- Each person's MAP emerges early in his or her life and stays constant.
- People tend to perceive their worlds through the eyes of their unique MAPs and attempt to perform jobs in a way that allows them to exercise their MAPs.
- When people work in jobs that play to their MAPs, they tend to excel, and when they are put into work that is contrary to their MAPs, they tend to become frustrated and generally perform poorly.

Art came to believe that each person has a core within that is foundational to who he or she is and that people are not blank sheets of paper to be written upon, or putty to be molded and shaped. He recognized the profound impact that life experiences have on individuals, but he also saw that despite the comfort or extremity of one's environment and experiences, the essence of a person's MAP remains constant.

He saw within each person something deeper and more meaningful than just skills and abilities. It was God's hand at work, he believed, and he backed it all up biblically.

He saw a pattern of behavior that continually repeated itself—that tried to repeat itself—despite the environment or living conditions it found itself within. This has significant implications for people and the organizations in which they worked.

As Art examined organizations, he saw that poor work performance, more often than not, was the result of people either being in jobs that did not fit them well or using their MAPs in ways that produced negative outcomes.

As Art listened to people review their lives, he realized that the essence of success and work satisfaction came as they embraced their MAPs, developed them, and made use of them.

When people spoke of their greatest successes, they revealed the MAPs that were unique to them. And when they spoke of failure and frustration, he saw that their MAPs were often denied expression and not allowed to flourish.

Something felt right to me about what Art was saying. My opportunity instinct antenna was vibrating. I wanted to learn more. His offices were located twenty miles from where I lived.

Art opened his files to satisfy my curiosity, and I dug into cases that were richly documented. I found it all quite absorbing. He gave me permission to try my hand at using his techniques and following his principles with the students and alumni I was counseling at Saint Joseph College. Whenever I could, I did short interviews using Art's techniques and tried to make observations about the MAPs each possessed.

The thing that repeatedly struck me was how accurate and simple his discoveries were. Yet within the simplicity were depth and complexity. Art was on to something, and I was being drawn in, deeper and deeper.

After more than forty years of working with MAPs, I have come to understand that when you engage in activity or get to a place or role that fits your MAP (your natural talent/giftedness), it can change your life for the better. It can lead to your feeling that your life has meaning and purpose. Once you know your MAP, you can use it to help direct your life and energy in directions that fit who you were designed to be.

Throughout this book, I use the following terms interchangeably MAP, giftedness, natural talent, natural strengths, natural abilities, motivational pattern, motivational strike zone, and nature. Here are three important things to know about MAPs:

1. The way to go about identifying your MAP is to make a list of ten to twenty achievements where you did something you enjoyed doing and felt you did well. The list should cover your entire life

and include achievements ranging from early childhood to recent years.

2. The exercise of making a list of achievements that cover you entire life, where you did something you enjoyed doing and felt you did well, is the first step in a process called The System for Identifying Motivated Abilities® (SIMA®). The second step is to describe in considerable detail how you accomplished what you did in each achievement.

3. The third step is to analyze those achievements to identify your MAP by looking for recurring themes. Your MAP is a picture of you in action when you are most highly motivated.

The process can be difficult, but the payoff can be enormous, even if you identify only some critical elements of your MAP.

For more detailed information about SIMA and the process for developing your MAP, please refer to my first book, *Managing Yourself, Managing Others: Learn How to Improve Effectiveness, Productivity, and Work Satisfaction*. The book describes in detail the SIMA process and MAP development, as well as various ways of applying your MAP. It also contains a bibliography of articles and other books about SIMA.

For Reflection and Discussion

1. Make a list of ten to twenty achievements that range over your life, where you did something you enjoyed doing and felt you did well. Don't discount achievements from childhood and teen years; they can be quite illuminating. Once you complete your list, evaluate and analyze your achievements by getting into the details of how you went about achieving those accomplishments. As best you can, try to identify the following five elements that combine to define your MAP:

    • Circumstances and conditions that you find energizing to work within. Some will trigger your motivation, some will sustain it, and some do both.

- Subject matter you are motivated to work with and through
- Abilities you derive great satisfaction using
- The ways you enjoy interacting with and relating to people
- Overarching central themes and results that seem to be inherent in those achievements that you find highly motivating and very much enjoy achieving

What common characteristics or themes do you see? What keeps recurring? When drawing conclusions, it is important to examine more than a few of the achievements on your list.

2. Have you purposely tried putting yourself into those kinds of settings where you can work with the subject areas you like to work with, under the conditions and circumstances that energize you, use the abilities you derive great satisfaction from using, interact with people in ways you enjoy, and in which you can realize the kinds of overarching central themes you find highly motivating and very much enjoy achieving? If not, why not?

SECTION 1

PART 2

Manage Your Giftedness

Your MAP can be a strength or a weakness. It can be a source for great joy or incredible despair, depending on how well you understand and manage it. When your MAP is combined with appropriate use and good stewardship, it feels remarkable because it is natural to how you have been designed.

The stories you are about to read in this section illustrate the importance of understanding and managing your MAP—your natural talent, your giftedness—and benefits from doing so. They also demonstrate that if you don't manage your MAP well, it can cause you and others problems and perhaps even lead you down paths and into holes that can become increasingly more difficult to escape.

CHAPTER 6

Unlock Your Giftedness

Have you ever been in sync with your giftedness? When you were doing something you felt born to do? How did it feel? Joyous? Glorious? Perhaps like putting on an old pair of shoes with an incredibly comfortable fit? Maybe like a warm embrace from a loved one?

When you are not using your MAP—your natural talent—in an appropriate manner, as intended, you can flounder about, unfocused, not realizing your potential and purpose.

In 2001, I wrote a book about the importance of finding your motivational strike zone, *Managing Yourself, Managing Others: Learn How to Improve Effectiveness, Productivity, and Work Satisfaction.* I revised the book in 2011, and again in 2015. It was quite a feat. Especially for me.

If you knew me as a kid, you would be saying to yourself, "Really? Darter? You've got to be kidding me! He'd be the last person I'd expect to write a book." And in 2002, much to my amazement, I was invited to speak before roughly 125 college and university presidents.

The message I wanted to convey and what that book is about is that we all have interests and abilities that come naturally to us. They drive us and motivate us to do our best, and this has implications for how we can most effectively manage and lead people and best manage ourselves.

By the time I wrote the book and was invited to speak before the college presidents, I had worked with many executives and organizations and some young people. I'm not saying I was always successful, but my message and work often had a positive impact. As a result, I was feeling quite good about myself, my reputation, and the personal success I had achieved.

Given my audience of educators—college presidents—and how I felt about myself, I thought it would be relevant to illustrate this message about natural interests and abilities and how we all have potential, purpose, and things that motivate us to do our best by telling a story about myself. But I didn't have the courage to stand before those college and university presidents and say what I really wanted to say.

I wasn't ready. I was still recovering—still avoiding—still creating an illusion about myself, about my image, and about my past that I didn't want anyone to know.

I kept looking at the biographies of the other main speakers and asking myself, "What am I doing here"? I felt I didn't belong—like an imposter who didn't want to be *outed*—who certainly wasn't going to *out* himself. My past was haunting and holding me down, and I wasn't strong enough to rise above it.

I had sold an image of success, of having always been successful. Opportunistically crafted, it focused on my advanced degrees; college teaching; and being an author, a company president, and a consultant to high-level executives. But I always omitted an important part. I never said a word about my beginnings and never, ever told anyone about its hold on me and my confidence.

What follows is the story I wanted to tell those college and university presidents but couldn't bring myself to tell.

This is a story about not giving up on people or yourself, about the importance of uncovering what motivates you to do your best, and how we can all affect the lives of others. It's taken from the world of academics, but the message, I believe, is universal.

I was expelled from elementary school in kindergarten, told in sixth grade that I was being allowed into the seventh grade "conditionally," and I barely graduated from high school, with a 65 average, at the bottom of my class, after having been left back, then passed on. My math and verbal SAT scores were around 800—not separate, but combined. On most national tests, I ranked in the 20th or 30th percentiles.

As a freshman in high school, I failed every subject I took. And when I say failed, I failed in style, like an 18 on my algebra final—can you imagine —and a 42 in general science. An academic I certainly wasn't.

When in school, I sat in the back of each class, folded my arms, and placed them on my desk, creating a pillow out of my folded arms, and slept —or hazed in and out—until the bell woke me. I then moved to my next class, where I did the same. Sitting up straight and following what the teacher was saying was nearly impossible for me to do.

On the days my mother worked, I sometimes cut school and hung out in a luncheonette called Joe's, where I gambled on pinball machines in the back. This kept me awake, and I was good at it. Sometimes those of us who cut school would go to my house, where I hosted a card game—carefully cleaning up before my parents returned from work. Cutting school and gambling continued throughout my high school years.

Aside from gambling, I played basketball. Most weekday nights, you would find me in a school gym, near my home, where I played basketball with the college kids. I loved playing against people who were much better than me. I wasn't much of a shooter, but I liked playing the point and getting the ball to the better shooters. I loved playing intense defense, and rebounding over guys who were bigger and stronger than me was—as the saying goes—to die for.

On the nights the gym wasn't open, sometimes, as the gym was closing from the afternoon session, I would take the cover from a book of matches, fold it in half, and place it against the back door to the gym, along the side of the door, so the door would close but not lock. When darkness arrived, I would sneak into the gym with my friends, Glenn and Joel. I did the same to the door for the athletic equipment room.

Just shooting hoops was not always enough. Sometimes we'd take the springboard out and place it below one of the baskets and engage in dunking competitions using a volleyball, imagining that we were much taller, imagining that we were in the NBA; watch me skying, getting rim, throwing down a tomahawk dunk! One evening, we found some tricycles in the boiler room, located next to the gym, and raced them through the hallways. On another night, we snuck into the main office and made announcements on the speaker system. We never got caught at any of this.

As I got older, I tried to stay awake in class—I wanted to stay awake in class—and often could do so only by playing a mental game of picking a number in the thousands and slowly counting toward that number, doing so in such a way that I would hit the number I selected simultaneously with the ringing of the bell that indicated the class period was over. I would start with 1, 2, 3, 4, and continue counting in my head until I counted to a number like 2,623, watching the clock on the wall so I would say the number in my mind just as the bell rang. This was not the best way to have a forty-five-minute class fly by, but if I didn't count and try to have the number I chose and the bell ringing come together simultaneously, I would drift off to sleep as I did in my freshman year.

I mastered my parents' signatures, producing absenteeism notes.

In my sophomore year, I had to take a parent to a conference with my guidance counselor. I hired a man who delivered cold cuts to Joe's luncheonette and with whom I gambled on the pinball machines in the back. He owed me money and paid off his debt by posing as my father.

I wasn't caught at this forging and posing until my last year of high school. After being caught, I was asked to take both my parents to a meeting with my guidance counselor. The counselor tossed me out of his office because I showed up with my sneakers untied, slouched in my chair, and displaying, as he put it, a bad attitude.

I attended summer school each summer, where it's difficult to fail, but I managed to fail.

To give you a better understanding of my academic record, I never took biology, chemistry, or physics and never took geometry, trigonometry, or calculus. On my third try, in my last year of high school, I passed Spanish 1, and I passed algebra on my fourth try—finally!

In addition to coming up with a number and counting as I had been doing to stay awake, by my third year in high school, I began making jokes in class when opportunities arose to do so. For example, when we were discussing Tom Sawyer and Huckleberry Finn, I took off my shoes and socks, rolled up my pants, and walked to the front of the class to get a pass to the lavatory. That gave me an adrenaline rush that kept me alert, at least for a while.

On several occasions, I was tossed from the classroom. They knew me quite well in the principal's office.

One teacher grew so frustrated with me that he told me to leave and not come back until I was ready to work. He wouldn't give me a hall pass; he just told me to leave, so I roamed the halls and hung out in a bathroom. I did return the next day with better behavior. He presented me no alternative, no wiggle room.

In my last year of high school, I passed an English IV course for which I received two credits instead of one, allowing me to graduate, on time—with my original classmates.

My wife, Diane, who graduated as the salutatorian from her high school, would have had absolutely nothing to do with me had she known me back then. She and others who have taught and administered in public schools tell me I couldn't have taken English IV without first passing English III and couldn't have received two credits for one course. No way! So I asked for a copy of my transcript, and there it was, with no explanation, other than an asterisk referring to the words "Modified Course." My feeling is that they wanted me out of the school because of my continual truancy, occasional classroom disruption, and, I suspect, a belief that I wasn't worth much effort.

I had started in what are called Regents' classes, designed for those who were going to attend college. I ended up in classes that were for *losers*, and that, I'll tell you, can assault your ego and do a job on your confidence.

One kid actually carved his initials on his left arm. I saw him do it, in class, in front of the teacher who chose not to stop him. The teacher knew better.

Despite being a lousy student, I oddly thought I would be going to college. It never occurred to me that I wasn't going to college. And that is where I headed, selecting a college from the back of a magazine, located in Scottsbluff, Nebraska, built in the middle of a cornfield, newly created and unaccredited, Hiram Scott College. The school remained in business for only four years.

I flew through Denver to get there. It had a twelve-to-one boy-to-girl ratio and thus was not a school I saw myself staying at for long. I quit after the first semester, returned home, and got a job in a supermarket stocking the dairy aisle.

My sister, Joan, who is seventeen years older than me and had already tried once to save me from myself, called and said, "You are not *not* going to college." She said she had enrolled me in Mohawk Valley Community College in Utica, New York. The school was on a trimester system, so in early March, I found myself in college again.

As you can imagine, I wasn't much of a student. I was not one to study or prepare. I did my assignments in a quick, sloppy, just-get-it-done manner, or I didn't do them at all.

First day, first class, English, twenty-seven students, all majoring in some sort of engineering, all guys except for one girl. I took my normal place in the rear of the class, second row, last seat—teacher, Steve Mocko.

After the traditional introductions, explanations, and syllabus distribution, Mocko gave us a short story to read. He asked what the story meant. People gave their opinions. To each thought that was expressed, Mocko said, "Possibly." Sometimes he asked people to expand on their opinions. He paced left and right in front of the class as he got some to think and express their thoughts.

To me, his acceptance of all the opinions people expressed seemed like a bunch of *bull*, so I decided to toss out the most asinine opinion I could think of just to see what he would do. He said, "Interesting. Expand on why you think so." I stumbled through an explanation. He listened, accepted, and moved on.

But there was something about him, something about his teaching style that I liked, that I connected with. Class over, reading assignment given. That evening I read carefully, more so than any assignment I had ever been given. I thought about what the author was trying to communicate.

At the beginning of the next class, Mocko stood before us and said, "I don't feel like teaching today. Would anyone like to teach?" I felt an urge in my body, within the core of my being, but no way was I going to raise my hand.

Like all the other students in that classroom, I sat in silence as he again asked if anyone would like to teach. Silence.

Steve Mocko then did something that changed my life. He strolled slowly down the second row to my seat at the back of the room. He stopped in front of my desk and said, "Mr. Darter, how would you like to teach today?"

I sat still, so very still, barely breathing, staring into his eyes, fighting the urge to jump up as I so wanted, immobilized by the fear of school and my lack of confidence. The classroom was not an arena I had ever had success in. It was not a competitive sport or a card game, battlefields that had become my comfort zones. I was so unsure. I didn't want to subject myself to more embarrassment, to more failure, but the urge to stand up and take the teaching mantle Mocko offered—offered to me—was very strong.

I awoke from the haze I was in—the fog—and took the teaching baton that he offered. I walked with cockiness to the front of the class. Each step I took sounded to me as loud as the beating of my heart and as large as the beads of sweat that were forming on the back of my neck.

I faced the class and asked what the story meant. I said "Possibly" to each opinion that was offered. I asked people to expand, imitating what I had seen Mocko do, including pacing left and right.

My mind was on fire. Thoughts flowed. Ideas jumped in and out. Colors were brighter. What people said grew louder and clearer. I was in the moment, in the flow, in a zone, in a way I had experienced only in sports and gambling. Time flew. There was no longer an uncontrollable compulsion to sleep, or the need to count or make jokes to stay awake.

When the class was over, Mocko asked me to come back to his office. We talked. He told me how he looked at my records, how he saw something in me, something in my records he could relate to.

Steve Mocko had a gift, and he used it to step into my life. He saw something inside me, something that I didn't see in myself. He reached in and pulled from me what he did, stimulating something, resident within, that I recognized but was not yet familiar with.

He started me on a journey that few would have expected. By doing so, he helped instill in me a foundational belief that we all have potential and purpose and an innate way of how we go about succeeding that is unique to us. It just needs to be uncovered and given the right soil, fertilizer, and sunlight to grow naturally, and the right gardener from time to time.

Steve Mocko awoke me from the sleep I was in as a student. I lifted my head off my arms to see another world, one that had been passing me by as I slept.

That was great teaching!

Steve Mocko, wherever you are, thank you.

I have come to realize that when I do something that comes naturally, it is hard to let it go, to dismiss it as a one-time freak occurrence. Giftedness needs to be released to grow and take its rightful place, and it should be capitalized on and managed well.

But I didn't have that awareness back then, at age eighteen, as I remained in the back of the classroom—safely hidden—occasionally participating in discussions that Steve Mocko led.

However, the feeling of standing before others had a firm hold on my emotional memory, and it was growing on its own, despite my resistance. I wanted to be up front—more in the action. I made my move to the front of a row in the safe arms of Steve Mocko's class. It went well.

This gave me confidence to move from the back to the front in other classes, with other professors. I committed myself to staying awake.

First came political science. There I was in the front row, sitting up straight, eyes wide open, determined that I would be successful. But within five minutes, my eyes began their slow descent, and my head soon followed, only to be jolted to brief attentiveness as I struggled to stay awake. My nemesis had not left.

"Bad move," I said to myself. "This isn't going to work. Tomorrow I'll return to the rear of the classroom, where I can fade in and out without being noticed." I now had to figure out a way to prevent embarrassment.

My strategy was to try forcing myself to stay awake by staring wide-eyed at the professor as he lectured. I kept looking at him, following him with my eyes and head as he moved about.

I noticed that as I stared at him, he often looked at me, seemed to talk to me, and each time he did, adrenaline released into my body, helping me remain awake. But it wasn't powerful enough to prevail over whatever it was that continually zapped my energy and attention as a student— whatever it was that continually caused me to doze off.

Perhaps as a defense against total collapse, or a last-ditch effort, as my eyes were closing, as my head was falling, and as my mind was shutting down, I raised my hand and asked a question. It was like a shot of caffeine pumping into my body, into my mind.

I replicated this whenever I found myself drifting—raising my hand and asking a question. I experimented in other classes, with other professors.

Not only was I making discoveries about teachers; I was discovering something critically important about myself and what I needed to do to remain awake and learn—what I needed to do to remain motivated and be successful as a student.

I unlocked the key to my learning. It began when I realized that I could influence the direction a professor took, the direction the class took, by the questions I asked.

Influencing others was intoxicating and felt natural to me. It was the same feeling I had standing in front of Steve Mocko's class, but there I was influencing others by raising my hand, asking questions, and listening for opportunities to do so.

I began doing homework and studying so that I was able to better influence, stockpiling knowledge for those moments—those opportunities when I could influence, facilitate, positively impact, and help. As I did, school and learning became more interesting, taking on a life of their own.

It wasn't until much later in my life, after I received my bachelor's degree, my master's in education, and my EdS degree in counseling, and after I started running a career planning and placement office and teaching career counseling in a graduate counseling program, that I met Arthur F. Miller Jr. (the founder of SIMA, the System for Identifying Motivated Abilities). He opened my eyes to understanding that we are all gifted, designed with a motivational strike zone that is unique to each of us, and the value in identifying and using it to more effectively manage ourselves and others and to achieve success.

It has taken me many years to truly understand one of Art's messages: we strengthen our souls by doing every day what we have been designed and gifted to do. When you are engaged in work and activity that fits your MAP—your natural talent, your giftedness—you will come closer to realizing the purpose of your life and your intended destiny—a journey that never seems to be the straight path you might think it should be, or would like it to be.

For Reflection and Discussion

1. To what extent do you believe you have a unique motivational strike zone that is at the core of your giftedness, and that when you tap into it in a positive manner, that you are moving closer to realizing the purpose of your life and your intended destiny?

2. What does it feel like to be engaged in work or an activity that is not motivating to you?

3. What does it feel like to be engaged in work or activity that is highly motivating for you?

CHAPTER 7

Find the Right People to Complement Your Nature

I don't think we are designed to go through life alone, without people who care about us, people who, if we allow them, help us to understand and manage our giftedness, help us develop our spirits and souls, and help us realize our life purpose and intended destiny. These are people whose giftedness, nature, and presence complement us—moderating us so we don't become out of control or self-defeating. The following story illustrates the importance of having such people in your life. If you don't have such people in your life, I urge you to seek them out and recognize their importance.

It was 5:00 p.m. on a winter day. Darkness had arrived, and the air was cold—the kind that penetrates jackets and gloves, to the bone. Rather than walk ten minutes down Derby and another five down Ibsen, I decided to take a shortcut and walk over the frozen water in the inlet. It would take only a few minutes to reach the warmth of my home. How I calculated that, I don't know. I had never taken that path home before. But the logic of an eleven-year-old adventurer could easily explain the rationale and decision.

I cut through someone's backyard, scrambled down the embankment, and slid onto the ice, slipping and sliding toward my destination, running as best I could on the ice, launching myself forward, sliding freely, arms spread out like a bird, landing on my butt, my side, back, or stomach, occasionally staying upright. It was fun and progress was being made—like life, in some ways, as I now reflect.

I straightened myself up somewhere past the middle of the journey, getting ready for another launch, when I heard a faint sound. I stopped to listen—quiet—then I heard it again, looked down, and saw the ice below beginning to crack, little white lines moving from a core, ever so slightly.

I'm not sure if I knew back then if what I did next was the right thing or if I just did it out of fear or luck. I lay on my stomach, spread my weight, and inched myself forward, toward the embankment on the other side.

As I got closer, I heard the cracking grow louder. I was within ten feet of solid ground. The cracks below were now encircling me. I stood up and pulled out an old knife I was carrying from my jacket pocket. I stepped forward with my left foot—I didn't sink. Then my right foot—the ice began caving in. I leapt using both feet—the ice crashed in below. I lifted myself into the air and caught the slope of the embankment, with my knife penetrating the dirt. I held on, preventing myself from tumbling back into the icy water. I used the knife to steady myself—slowly pulling up to safety.

It was scary but exhilarating. There was something about the gamble, the risk, the challenge, the unknown, and the adrenaline rush that attracted me. I could have been a statistic on the evening news—"Boy falls through frozen ice and dies"—but I wasn't.

I didn't realize it back then, but there is a restlessness inside me that needs to be fed by risk, a gamble, the challenge of facing an unknown, something intense. It has led me to do things that, let's just say, I would be well-advised not to have done.

As a teenager and young man in the 1960s, I would often go to high-stakes poker games ($1, $2, $4, or pot limit at the end, for those of you who know about such things) with little money in my pocket, occasionally with no more than $25, knowing I had to win one of the first hands I stayed in. The unknown, the risk–reward, the intensity was something I longed for—unaware that I was feeding the monster inside. And if I lost, I would try borrowing money to continue playing. Most weekends, gambling became the centerpiece of my life, with hundreds of dollars flowing to or away from me, taking my emotions along for the ride.

During my college years, I was willing to try most things, rarely thinking of consequences, often wondering why, not wanting to waste the opportunity and freedom, both of which I was ill-prepared to control.

When I returned home the summer after my freshman year in college, I went on a gambling losing streak, losing most of what I was earning—money I desperately needed to help pay for my college education—night after night, playing poker with people I had been gambling with for years—high school friends. One night, one of them took me aside and told me to leave, that they were cheating me. He said they were shooting heroin, and I was one source of the funds they needed to do so.

I convinced my father that I needed to get away. He asked me, "To where?" and "Why?" I didn't know where. But I knew why. I lied about both. He let me take the family car. We had only one. I was not aware of the sacrifice he made—how he got to work, went shopping, or did other activities that required an automobile.

I drove and drove, finally ending up in Providence, Rhode Island, where I showed up at the home of someone I knew. He had his own apartment in the ghetto, surrounded by prostitutes and drug addicts. I don't know why I ended up there. He was dealing drugs. I stayed the night and left the next day, ending up in Utica, New York, staying the night with another person I knew. There was no comfort, no peace of mind. I was lost, so I headed back to Long Island, to my parents' home. There was nowhere else to go.

Feeling restlessness is forever present in me. Learning to quell it or use it productively became a life challenge, but I certainly didn't know it at the time.

I would drive to places I had never been, without a map, often with no sense of where I was heading or why, and see what would happen, what I would experience, dealing with the unknown, but never feeling quite comfortable. I would smoke or swallow what was offered, go to places with anyone who asked, sometimes waking up in strange surroundings, vaguely remembering the events that led me there.

I attended three colleges, and at each I kept feeling and wondering if I should be someplace else. After graduating from college, I moved from Oswego to Long Island to Syracuse and back to Long Island, all in the space of less than one year. I had little direction and no *home* to connect with or to ground me, but considerable energy, unfocused and squandered. Then I met Diane in the spring of 1972, and my life changed.

It was a Friday night, 10:30, and I was moving like a hungry lion from one room to the next within my parents' five-room apartment. I had heard an advertisement for the Pub Ivanhoe, located in Glen Cove. It was a one-hour drive from where I was. It was nearly midnight when I walked through the door of the pub.

The place was crowded with wall-to-wall people, smoke, drinks, and a loud band. I met some guys from Canada. They were interested in meeting the girls who were behind me. I'm not shy. I tapped the shoulder of the short, cute one and introduced myself. This was Diane. All I saw were big, blue eyes and a radiant smile. I was hooked, smitten. She became my focus, my target.

She was shy, a bit hesitant. I was bold. She was a junior high math teacher. I told her I was a private detective, that I owned a gun, that I followed people, and that my current case involved following a husband who was cheating on his wife. She was enthralled—mesmerized, I thought. Months later, she told me that she knew I was giving her a line—"full of shit," she actually said—but she liked my creativity and smile.

We danced a bit. I asked if she wanted a drink. "A Coke," she said. I drank a 7-Up. We talked. She told me how she had been living in a house with friends. About how there was a break-in while all were sleeping. About a guy who tried to rape one of her friends and how they fended him off, made a dash for the car, drove to the police station with curlers in their hair, wearing PJs and bathrobes, and now they were all living in their parents' homes again. The police caught the guy. He was the mayor's son.

She told me how driving to a nightclub like that, by herself, was something she had never done before. I listened.

Her friends said they were leaving, that it was time to go. She started to leave but hesitated. I asked if she would like to get something to eat, to continue talking. Cautiously she said yes. We drove to an all-night diner and ordered bacon, eggs, toast, juice, and tea.

She told me about her mother, father, brother, and sisters; about attending Catholic elementary and high schools; and about graduating as the salutatorian of her class. She told me about her childhood—playing sports, attending church, being the oldest daughter her mother depended on, and being a rock. I listened. She didn't hold back. She told me about attending college at the State University of New York at Oneonta, being president of her sorority house, and winning the Greek of the Year Award for leadership, service, and academic performance; about herself, her thoughts, who she was, and who she wanted to be; and how she changed herself. As she talked, I grew incredibly calm inside.

We looked at our watches. Hours had passed. It was now after 3:00 a.m. She was concerned about driving home safely and asked if I would follow her, to make sure she arrived home safely. I agreed, thinking the evening was going to end well, the way any sex-craved twenty-two-year-old male would want.

After twenty minutes, Diane pulled her blue Ford Maverick into a driveway. I pulled my old maroon Mercury Cougar in behind. I was excited, anticipating. She got out of her car and walked to the driver's window of my car. I rolled the window down. She thanked me for following her home, kissed my cheek, asked me to call her, and quickly disappeared up the driveway and into the back door of the house. I was stunned. Misread that one.

She was continuously on my mind. I called and asked her out for a date: "The whole day," I said.

I told her it was a surprise when she asked, "Where are we going? What will we be doing?" I added that she should bring an extra set of clothes. When she got in the car, she didn't have extra clothes.

"Where are we going?" she asked a bit more sternly, the way teachers can, giving you the *teacher's* look.

"Out of state—to Connecticut—first to Mystic Seaport and then to dinner with my sister and her husband," I responded, somewhat confidently, as men try to do in these situations.

Mystic Seaport was delightful. I had seen an advertisement and wanted to go see it. We walked on and off old shipping vessels; viewed oars, anchors, clothes, and all sorts of items; listened to seafaring tales; and looked at the stars in the planetarium, where I snuck a quick nap.

On the way back, we stopped off in New Haven. We walked around Yale University, ending in a courtyard that had a lot of people milling about and others looking out windows from the four buildings that enclosed the courtyard.

There was a platform in the middle of the courtyard with several tables and chairs. We were intrigued but not aware of what was going to happen or had happened.

We heard sirens in the distance that grew louder. The gates to the courtyard opened, and in drove two ambulances. The back doors opened, and out jumped ten guys dressed in weird outfits. There are no words to describe those outfits. The men leapt onto the platform. One group jumped around, pumping their raised arms and fists in the air to the cheers of half the crowd. Then the other group did the same to the cheers of the other half.

A keg of beer was carried onto the stage. Five of the weirdly dressed guys sat on chairs on one side of the table, and the other five weirdly dressed guys sat on the other side of the table. Beer was poured into the cups before them, and the drinking contest began, with all the hollering, whooping, and beer guzzling you could imagine.

I held Diane's hand, periodically glancing to watch her—study her—her smile, eyes, face, and movements. She lit up, and I was incredibly calm inside. My restlessness quelled.

Afterward, we drove to my sister's house in Stamford. But I never called to see if she and her husband were available. It never dawned on me to do so. They weren't home.

On our second date, I asked Diane if she wanted to smoke a joint. "Good stuff," I said.

She said no and asked me, "Why?"

I didn't have a good answer.

In June, when her school year was over, Diane drove cross-country with a friend—a trip they had been planning for a long time. We had known each other for only two months when she drove off.

For six weeks, Diane and her friend, Joanie, traveled west to Chicago, the Dakotas and Mount Rushmore; to Wyoming, down to New Mexico and Carlsbad Caverns; to San Francisco, Los Angeles, and San Diego; and to many places in between. She sent me letters, not knowing if I cared, not knowing if I was still interested in her.

Mostly she and Joanie slept under the stars, in a tent, at campsites. In a few locations, they stayed with graduate students who were friends of someone Diane taught with. In Los Angeles, they stayed with a person from India who was from the Brahmin class. He read their futures. He told Joanie that she would inherit a lot of money and marry someone overseas. Both came true. He told Diane that within a year, she would be married. She laughed. Less than five months after she returned, we were married. He also told her that the person she was marrying would bring her closer to God. If she understood then what I believed about God and religion, she would not have married me.

It was November, and I asked, "What are you doing this weekend?"

"Why?"

"Let's get married."

She said yes, but told me that there were things we had to do, like get a marriage license and plan the wedding. I was oblivious. I hadn't given any of this much thought. Asking her to marry me felt right, though. I had been accepted into graduate school and didn't want to move away without her. The distance, I felt, would cause the fire to extinguish. Six weeks later, we were married.

Diane is logical, analytical, and not one to make quick, spontaneous, rash decisions. But she did that night when I asked her to marry me.

Diane's parents didn't like the decision. One of her sisters was getting married in June. That wedding had been planned well in advance. "Why? Why now? Why him? Can't you wait until after Chris's wedding?" The dependable oldest daughter held her ground, despite the emotional onslaught and violation to her own sense of logic.

When we told my parents, they asked Diane, "Do you know what you are getting into? Are you sure?" They loved me, but they liked Diane and felt that she should have fair warning about me.

Diane and I fit. We are complementary puzzle pieces. At times, I think our souls have forever been connected, that God and fate presented an opportunity, and that at that moment in the Pub Ivanhoe, our souls recognized each other, reaching out to connect, without either of us being consciously aware of it.

Until that happened, I was on the wrong side of life, slipping and sliding on ice that was starting to crack—unfocused, unhappy, restless, and adrift. Then, like finding an island in uncharted waters, or an oasis in a desert, Diane appeared and became the antidote—her presence, giftedness, and nature calming the monster inside, helping to free me from my internal trap.

For Reflection and Discussion

1. One's MAP can be a strength, or it can become a liability if it is not understood and managed well. If you don't manage your MAP well, it becomes more difficult to realize the purpose of your life and intended destiny. One factor in making sure your motivational pattern doesn't lead you astray is to have one or more people in your life whose nature and presence complement you—moderating so you don't become out of control, self-defeating, or self-destructive. If you have such people in your life, who are they?

2. How have they helped you?
3. What is it about them and their natural talents that you need, that fit well with you, that serve as a balance?
4. Do you resist such people?
5. If you do resist them, why?

CHAPTER 8

Know When to Rely on the Natural Talents of Others

Have you ever tried to do something you are not good at, and no matter how much you tried, you just couldn't do it well because you lacked the natural talent—the needed giftedness? How did your poor performance and perhaps sense of incompetence cause you to feel about yourself? What words would you use to capture those feelings? Has this ever happened to you, despite your education, intelligence, and maybe even specific training? Do you recall the frustration? Perhaps the pain? Did doubt creep in? Did it slam you? Could you just brush it off?

The following story further demonstrates the importance of managing yourself and your MAP. It points out that you will have a greater chance for success and satisfaction in life, and a greater chance of realizing your purpose and intended destiny, if you learn to rely on the giftedness of others. Doing so will be good for your psyche. And you will see that it is good for the psyche of those who have the needed natural talents. You have not been designed to be good at everything.

This fundamental truth has relevance to how you manage your personal life and your work life and how you can assist others as they strive to find meaning and purpose in their lives.

My dad was handy. He could build, fix, and repair anything. He built a family room and garage, adding to the house I grew up in. When I decided to see if I could somersault off the dresser onto my bed, putting my feet through the wall, he turned the giant hole I created into built-in shelving and bookcases. When my mother began painting, in her late sixties, he lovingly constructed picture frames for each of her masterpieces. When Diane and I first got married, he made us a tiled coffee table, and when he visited, he used what few tools I owned to make repairs to our home that I had neglected. No one taught him how to be good at building and fixing things; he just knew how to do it, how to figure it out. It came naturally to him. It was part of his giftedness and design.

When I was a kid, my dad built a garage for our home, and afterward he built a large workbench and installed pegboard on which to hang the multitude of tools he owned. Next to his workbench, he built a tiny workbench for me, with pegboard backing, on which I could hang my tools. Underneath my workbench, he would toss odd pieces of wood he no longer needed. They were mine to hammer, nail, and construct to my heart's content.

The problem was, I didn't know what I was doing. No matter what I tried to build, it came out so bad that even my dad's kind words couldn't overcome the frustration each attempt produced. Occasionally he would show me how to do something, but whatever competence I had in building and constructing would not emerge. It was either nonexistent or buried so deeply that unconventional methods would have been needed to extract what little talent existed.

The image, though, of being competent in building, fixing, and repairing things is with me, gained through the connection with my father. It is what men do—what husbands and fathers are supposed to do.

During the early years of our marriage, when Diane and I settled into each of the apartments we lived in, I took it upon myself to hang the curtain rods. Each time, without fail, they came out crooked. Diane would try to make suggestions, but I shut her down. This was a man's job, my job, and she had no place, no standing, and no opinion. So she stood silently, watching me make mistake upon mistake. And the curtain rods I hung remained crooked.

I was similarly incompetent when it came to putting the screen into the front door of our newly purchased condominium. It just wouldn't go in properly, so I took a screwdriver to force it in—force being my natural default position and solution to all building and fixing problems. The screwdriver slipped, punching a hole in the screen.

When things broke, I would look at the manuals to figure out what to do. It would usually take me hours to do what may have taken someone with any modicum of ability five minutes to do, and I was lucky if, after all that time, the item ever got fixed.

Putting together newly purchased items rarely went any better. Following a manual (Step 1, Step 2…) was as frustrating to me as trying to learn a foreign language. And in those situations when words were replaced by pictures, I was totally lost. In those early years of marriage, I broke many items, or made them worse, in my attempts to build, fix, assemble, or repair something.

Throughout my life, when conversations turned to technical matters about how to fix, repair, or build something, my mind would wander. I tried to listen. I tried to understand. I tried to be interested.

This all became a laughing matter, with me leading the jokes and making fun of myself and my incompetence. Jokes ease the tension, help get one through, but they don't erase the pain of enduring incompetence, of feeling that you are not measuring up to who you want to be—who you see yourself being.

It was into our fourth year of marriage and our fifth move when I began to realize that Diane was better at building, fixing, and repairing than I was. It started with another curtain rod I was hanging. As usual, it was not going well. As usual, the tape measure was off, the level was not working properly, and the floor and ceiling were not straight.

"Let me try?" Diane asked firmly but respectfully.

"We should have never bought this place. Go ahead, see if you can do it," I said out of anger and frustration.

A few minutes later, I was following her instructions, becoming her pair of hands. Result: for the first time since we were married, our curtain rods were straight.

This opened the door, and there was no turning back. The taillight in my car wasn't working. The manual said to change the bulb. I bought a new bulb at the auto parts store. For forty-five minutes, I tried to change that bulb. I couldn't figure out how to get the old one out, let alone put the new one in. Diane arrived home. My enormous frustration had already filled the air.

"Do you want help?" she asked.

"This stupid thing just won't come out."

She looked at the manual and at the bulb, stuck her hand in, and out popped the old bulb. Less than a minute later, the new bulb was in place.

When spring came and it was time to put the screen into the screen door, I asked Diane to help, finally accepting my own limitations and incompetence. Equally important, I was recognizing her natural ability and competence, enabling it to develop, along the way easing the frustration we both felt. Manuals and instructions became her domain, as did fixing, repairing, and assembling. Sometimes I would try to do something on my own, often returning to her. She would point out what I missed or didn't follow correctly.

I vividly recall trying to reassemble an old bike I bought for our son, Kevin. I decided to take it apart and clean it. There I was, with parts strewn over the floor. Kevin was watching me, anticipating, excited, asking how long, and I was sweating profusely, angry at myself, disappointed in myself, wanting more than anything to come through, to deliver, to reassemble that bike, to be like my father as my son watched and waited.

As morning gave way to afternoon and afternoon to evening, I sat cross-legged on the floor, teary-eyed, wondering what to do with the parts I had left over, wondering where they belonged, knowing I had to start over again.

Incompetence turning into panic can freeze the mind, immobilize the will, and deaden the spirit. Will and determination, I have learned, can prevail, but they are sometimes not enough. Success comes with maturity as you understand and better manage yourself.

"Diane, I need your help." I said. It was the assistance she had offered earlier that I had resisted. Egos sometimes die slowly.

A few years later, I flew to St. Louis for a series of meetings. I got into my rental car and drove to the first meeting location. I was running late. I parked the car and pulled at the ignition key, but it wouldn't come out. I wondered, "What do I do? Do I lock the car door or leave it open? The key is in the ignition; someone could steal the car. But if I lock the door, I can't get back in." I left the door unlocked. I asked the secretary to call Hertz and explain the problem, and I went into my meeting. One hour later, the secretary handed me the keys and explained that there was a little release button you have to press to take the key out of the ignition.

All day long, I went from meeting to meeting, telling my story to anyone who would listen—how idiotic it is to have a release button. "Stupid, stupid, stupid!" I emphasized.

That evening when I called Diane, I couldn't wait to tell her my key story and about the stupid release button. When I told her that the key wouldn't come out of the ignition, she immediately asked, "Did you look for a release button?"

"No!" I yelled. "Why would you think there is a release button?"

"Have you ever had a key not come out of the ignition?" she calmly asked me.

"No, but...," I said, trying to rationalize away my incompetence. She continued, "So the first thing I would look for is some sort of release button."

This is how her mind works. She is an organized, focused problem solver, and I love this about her; it's 180 degrees opposite the way my mind naturally works.

She can easily become hooked on trying to figure out an answer or a solution to a problem. For example, she bought a new printer and set it up, but it kept feeding pages—endlessly. The manual had no answers. "Call Hewlett Packard," I keep saying as she tried various solutions. She didn't call HP; she figured it out on her own.

In another illustration, we went out to dinner with another couple. Fran told a riddle to be figured out. I hate this riddle stuff unless I'm the one who presents the riddle—the one in a sparking, instigating role. After a few minutes, I changed the subject, purposely distracting all from the riddle. When we got home from the night out, Diane immediately went to her computer and sent an email.

"To whom?" I asked.

"I'm emailing Fran the answer to the riddle," she said.

The problem to be solved—the riddle—got into her head, and she couldn't let it go. She was compelled to figure it out.

The contrast between how our minds work is clear.

Several years back, we hired a cleaning service to clean our home. The next morning, I woke up and noticed that the ring around the large front left burner was missing. I began looking for it. It was not in the garbage or in any of the cabinets. Where could it be? I imagined that the cleaning person placed it on the back of the stove and that it fell behind the stove.

I started to shimmy the stove away from the wall. I was concerned because it is a gas stove, and I didn't know how it is connected to the gas line. I was worried about pulling it too hard and causing a gas leak.

I got a flashlight and knelt on the counter and stove, trying to see if that missing stove ring had fallen behind. As I was doing that, Diane came into the kitchen. She had just woken up; it was 5:45 a.m. Maybe I woke her up as

I kept moving the stove. She exasperatedly said to me what she usually says in these situations: "What are you doing?"

I explained that the stove ring was missing, how I looked for it in the garbage and in all the cabinets, that the cleaning person may have stolen the ring—why she would, I didn't know—how it may have been placed on the back of the stove and may have fallen behind, which is why I had begun to shimmy the stove out, but I was worried about disconnecting the gas line, so I got the flashlight, and I was looking to see if it fell back there, behind the stove.

Diane looked at me with her usual amusement in these situations. She then looked at the stove. Bleary-eyed, tired, barely awake, no coffee yet, her mind half working, she took her pinky nail and lifted up the missing stove ring, which was sitting on top of the stove ring on the other large burner.

"How did you know that?" I asked, both frustrated and amazed. Before she could answer, I put myself into her way of thinking. The logical solution, I realized, is that the burner ring was too big to just disappear, so it must have been camouflaged, and the logical place to look was on the other burner. She nodded her head in agreement.

There was no conscious thought process that she went through to figure out a solution to this problem; it just came to her naturally, effortlessly.

I thought, "This is what natural ability is, what giftedness is. It comes naturally without thinking about it." This is in contrast to a *can do* skill—a skill one can learn.

I thought, "If I come down tomorrow morning and see the stove ring missing, I will look at the other burner, having learned to do so. But if a knob was missing, I would not know where to begin. I would again be incompetent in my attempts."

Yes, I can force myself, discipline myself, to think as Diane does, as a logical problem solver when dealing with building, fixing, and technical matters, but I have to slow down and concentrate on doing so. Sometimes it works. Often it doesn't. It is just not part of my MAP, but it is part of Diane's MAP.

Yesterday I fixed a leaking toilet—after Diane figured out where the leak was coming from. And truth be told, I had previously seen a plumber tighten those kinds of nuts.

Diane and I balance each other, rely on each other, and are stronger together than we are alone. She frees me to concentrate on what I do well. When I do, I am more successful, life is more satisfying and meaningful, and I feel more in sync with who I was designed and destined to be. And at times, I do the same for her.

For Reflection and Discussion

1. When should you rely on the natural talent of others—giftedness that you don't have?

2. How have you done things that prevented others from developing and using their natural talent—their giftedness?

3. How have you done things that helped others develop and use their natural talent—their giftedness?

CHAPTER 9

Take Advantage of Opportunities that Fit Your MAP

Life presents many opportunities. Some fit, some don't. Some lead you astray; some move you down the right path. All afford you the opportunity to learn, grow, and develop. There is risk to any decision you make and any direction you select, but if you remain true to your giftedness, your natural talent—your MAP—you will have a greater chance to achieve meaning, success, and satisfaction in your life and significantly improve your odds of realizing the purpose of your life and fulfilling your intended destiny.

The following story illustrates how important it is to find work that fits with your MAP. If you understand the kinds of opportunities that fit with your MAP, it becomes easier to recognize and pursue them. If you don't understand your MAP and what you find highly motivating, there is a greater chance that you will feel frustrated and unsatisfied, or perhaps worse.

I exited the taxicab as if I were floating on air, breezed through the check-in process, found a telephone booth, and called Diane, who was caring for Kevin and Katie, in our older Cape Cod-style home we had purchased several years earlier.

"I can't believe it! I got it!" I exclaimed with emotion that couldn't contain itself.

"Got what?" Diane asked calmly, clearly tired.

"I made the sale! The commission alone is worth almost three thousand dollars!"

It was money we desperately needed to remain in our home. Money we needed to continue, what seemed to me, an improbable ride, one that I felt could end at any moment.

I sat in a chair by the gate where my flight was to depart, too excited to work and not wanting to let go of the feeling and glow. I thought back: at that moment, at thirty-six years of age, I still had trouble believing it was all real. My mind drifted to an earlier time in my life.

After graduating from college in 1971, I headed back to Long Island, to my parents' home. I wasn't sure where else to go. I answered an advertisement for a job with a large New York City bank and was invited in for an interview. I took the Long Island Railroad into Penn Station and then the subway to lower Manhattan. I walked into the office building and rode up the elevator to the Personnel Office. My hair was long and didn't fit the setting. Neither did I, in my dress pants, buttoned-down shirt, and tie. I didn't get the job.

The thought of a long commute by train into New York City, and then a subway into lower Manhattan, felt unbearable. The next day I left, riding a bus to Syracuse.

I moved in with two friends, Stu and Gerry, who lived in a one-bedroom apartment in an oddly shaped triangular building behind the bus terminal. Gerry worked as a machinist; Stu as a Howard Johnson's cook.

Out of kindness and a desire to be supportive, my sister, Joan, sold me her older Ford Cougar car. "You don't need to pay me," she said, "until you get a job." I quickly did so after answering an ad for a manager's job with a regional retail men's clothing chain, which was opening a new store. It was a small store, and I was the manager and the only employee.

I went on a buying trip to New York City with the two brothers who owned the chain of stores and helped select merchandise that my generation would like. I had ideas but little natural talent for fashion and anticipating what would sell.

Diane is still amused by the thought of me as a buyer of clothing and as a manager of a men's clothing store—shorts, jeans, a T-shirt or polo, and sneakers are more to my liking.

The store was located in a strip shopping center, not far from a high school. New merchandise was placed in the store, along with unsold clothing from other stores.

Stu, Gerry, and I moved to a three-bedroom apartment in North Syracuse.

Retail work does not suit me well, but at the time, I didn't know it. The first clue emerged shortly after I began working, when I discovered that I was inept at putting shirts back into the original packaging after using one for a display. You know the ones, with cardboard backing, tissue paper, and pins to hold the shirt in place.

Despite repeated attempts and intense care on my part, the cardboard would bend in ways that were not intended, the crinkly tissue paper would stick out like a poorly tucked-in shirt, pins would end up in the wrong places, buttons would look crooked even though they were inserted into the correct button holes, the shoulders had a sagged and angled appearance, and the folds I made resulted in the shirt being either too big or too small for the plastic wrapping.

I could spend an entire day trying to get a shirt neatly back into its original wrapping. As a result, I stopped changing displays. The owners noticed. They insisted that I continue to change displays. My solution: always use a display shirt that was my size, and then purchase it.

The store was busy in the evening and on weekends, but few customers came in at other times. I was incredibly bored.

One day, several high school students came into the store when they should have been in school.

"Is there no school today?" I asked.

"We're cutting school."

"Why?"

"It's boring."

I let them hang out in the store that day, and the next time they cut school, and the time after that. It was as if I had placed breadcrumbs to draw in hungry animals—whenever they cut school, they would show up. Maybe it was out of empathy; after all, I could relate to their distaste for school. Or perhaps it was a way to deal with my own boredom.

We stood around, bored, talking, mostly about their lives—drugs, drinking, abuse, divorce, parental rules, yelling—and about their futures, all topics that held my interest. I listened and asked questions. I sat on a stool. They remained standing.

"Can I sit on the floor?" one of them eventually asked.

I paused for a moment and then said hesitantly, "OK, but get up quickly if someone comes into the store."

It didn't take long for me to feel awkward sitting on a stool while they were sitting on the floor. So I pushed the stool back and sat on the floor with them. All of us sat in a circle, legs crossed, talking about their lives and the issues they faced. I asked my questions, listening, totally absorbed, and becoming oblivious to one of the owners, who had walked in through the back door and was now staring at us, but mostly glaring at me.

"What's going on?" he asked angrily in a violated, authoritarian tone.

"I'm building customer relationships," I said quickly with a smile, in my defense.

"Get out! You're fired! I'll send your final paycheck in the mail!"

Not a good beginning to my post-college career.

I needed to earn money and to obtain a new job quickly.

I arrived at the offices of Mutual Benefit Life Insurance Company to see Ed Markson, the general agent for the Syracuse region. I knew nothing about life insurance.

Ed asked me a few questions, but mostly he talked and talked and talked. And I listened and listened and listened. At the end of two hours, Ed offered me a job as a sales agent, saying, "Anyone who could listen as well as you has to be a good salesman."

What he didn't know was that I was too unsure to know what to say, so each time he stopped talking, I asked a question, my mind energized by the need to figure out what was important to focus on and what to ask next.

I accepted the job.

I lasted six months as a life insurance agent. I should have known the fit was not good when, within a few weeks of starting, I went to Mutual Benefit Life's home office in Newark, New Jersey, for training.

Standing before my group of new hires was a Million Dollar Round Table agent who told how he always wanted to own a Rolls Royce.

"Now I own one, and so can you," he emphasized from the podium. We all applauded.

I thought about how the previous year I had been demonstrating against the Vietnam War, rules, regulations, restrictions, capitalism, and American society and culture—which I didn't understand and certainly didn't appreciate at the time. And now, there I sat, the owner of a suit, several white shirts, several ties, and a pair of wingtip shoes, listening to a successful life insurance agent tell me that I, too, could own and drive a Rolls Royce.

I made several sales and discovered that I liked earning large sales commissions.

The tension of venturing into the unknown through cold-call selling satisfied a visceral need I seemed to have, but I saw and felt a pattern to my life taking shape—little of which felt right. I began questioning: Did I really want to be like that Rolls Royce-driving agent?" I felt myself changing in ways I didn't like—a poorly defined and not-understood transition—fighting assumptions and a self-image that needed adjustment.

I felt like I was *selling out,* a phrase coined by that time period and generation. I grew restless.

I began staying up late each evening, smoking marijuana, and playing the addicting board game Risk (how coincidental and appropriate the name).

As my energy drained, my sales dropped off. I became a mess and fell even further—my demise enhanced by my confusion and an inability to understand what was happening and how to counter it.

I fled, returning once again to the safety of home, to regroup and think things through, I would say, but I didn't have any of that awareness. All I knew is that I was hurting and a mess, and I needed to flee. Only one place felt like the right place to be, and that was home.

I sat in the airport after making that sale to Monsanto, which involved working with PhD scientists and engineers, which itself was surprising because I had taken few science courses and had limited interest in technology. I thought about how, after returning home, I had worked as a stock boy at a Shoe Town store organizing the men's stockroom, which had many older shoes out of boxes, on the floor, and stuffed into openings on the shelves. How one day a salesperson didn't show up and the manager asked me to work the sales floor—and how I knew that the red, green, and blue dots on the boxes represented points leading to prizes for selling those shoes. They were mostly top name brands, discounted to a fraction of their original cost, but there were only a few sizes in each style. I thought about how I sold a lot of those older shoes that day and was asked to move out of the stockroom and onto the sales floor.

I thought of a job I had in a factory and another selling Kirby vacuum cleaners in graduate school, a paid one-year internship as a counselor at the State University of New York at Purchase, and then in July 1975, I was hired as the director of career planning and placement at Saint Joseph College in West Hartford, Connecticut.

One year later, I met Arthur F. Miller, Jr., and my life would forever change. Shortly after, he asked if I wanted to work part-time on an hourly basis, helping counsel executives who had lost their jobs—individuals to whom People Management Inc. (Art's company at the time) was hired to provide outplacement services.

My role involved calling each job hunter weekly, after they completed the formal part of the program, to keep them on track and to provide whatever job-hunting advice I could.

In weekly conversations, I would verbally walk each person through his or her week's efforts. "Who did you see? Who did you call? What did you say? What did they say? How did you respond?" I would listen for lost opportunities, provide needed advice, and suggest angles to pursue and tactics to try.

One of my first outplacement clients was the Head of Ventures for Allied Chemical. I spent one hour getting to know him and then walked down the hall to ask Jim Cunningham, who ran the outplacement service, what a venture was. He explained. I felt that I was in over my head. Jim told me not to worry. But I did.

Feeling in over my head became the ongoing norm when Art asked me to counsel executives, by telephone, who had completed their MAPs. I was twenty-six years old.

My first MAP counseling client was a research and technology executive from Dow Chemical. I knew nothing about the chemical research world. I kept telling myself that I was knowledgeable about job hunting and this motivational pattern stuff. It was both scary and exhilarating. My senses were keen.

I felt like a kid, peeking around a closed curtain on a stage for the first time, in awe of what I was seeing and learning. I felt energized by the challenge of taking what I knew and was learning from listening to these executives and applying it on the spot, using my instincts.

My lack of knowledge and feelings of being in over my head and out of my league emerged even stronger when Art gave me the MAP of someone, asked that I read it, and put thought to career ideas. He asked me to show up at 8:00 a.m. on Friday in the company conference room.

When I walked into the room, there were several People Management professionals, all of whom I recognized, and Henry Roberts, who was the chairman and CEO of Connecticut General Life Insurance Company. He was going to leave his post as CEO and wanted our collective thoughts about his next steps. He was a big fan of Art and People Management and had been through the SIMA and MAP process earlier in his career.

"Ambassador" was the first suggestion someone made. I was in a daze.

I thought about how three years earlier, I was a stock boy at Shoe Town. I didn't say a word. I just listened, following the advice my former brother-in-law once told me: "No fish ever got caught with his mouth shut."

In 1979, shortly before my thirtieth birthday, Art asked me to join People Management as a full-time employee.

By the time of Art's offer, I was being given outplacement assignments, MAP-based counseling assignments, and an occasional retained executive search assignment, whenever one came the company's way. And I was still working at the college and also teaching a career counseling course in the college's graduate school.

I accepted Art's job offer. The decision was a good one. By 1984, I was consistently earning in the $40,000 to $60,000 range, feasting on the sales of others who produced the business.

Art and then-president of People Management, Bob Gattorna, called me into Bob's office and explained that the outplacement business, through which most of my compensation was being earned, was not where the future of People Management's profits would be. They explained that providing outplacement services had become a commodity business with lowball pricing taking over. They wanted me to take over and build up the executive search practice, which had dwindled to almost no search assignments.

They went on to explain that I would not be asked to do any more outplacement counseling, nor would I be assigned much MAP-based counseling. They wanted me to concentrate on selling and doing retained executive search work.

My $20,000 base-salary compensation would not change, but as an incentive, they offered me a greater percentage of revenue from the executive-search work I sold.

I had little experience selling retained executive search services or any consulting. I had tried a bit with minimal success. I had been handed so much business to work on that there was no need to try to sell. My world changed. It was the spring of 1984.

By December 1984, I had not made a sale, and Diane and I owed

$14,000 on our credit card. We weren't sure where our next mortgage payment was coming from, and some bills sat in a pile, unpaid. Our options were limited. Diane offered to go back to teaching math or to take some other job she could find. It's not what we wanted. I was panicked. My nails were bitten to their cores, and my stomach was in continual knots.

In late December, Bob Gattorna asked that I call Roger Abate, who was a sales executive in the Group Insurance Division at the Massachusetts Mutual Life Insurance Company. When I left that meeting, I made my first executive search sale, and it eventually led to another and another. But it was one sale at one company and one client. The financial hole that Diane and I were in was deep. I needed more sales and more clients.

In the early 1980s, Art introduced me to Bill Campbell, who was head of human resources for the Research Center for Monsanto. Every four months or so, I would call Bill. He always took my call, but no sales ever resulted.

On this one call, I sensed an uneasy tone in his voice and asked him what was wrong. He told me how he was charged with identifying people with PhDs in science and engineering who had potential to become business executives.

"I can help you do that," I told him.

"How?" he asked, now paying closer attention to things I had alluded to in previous telephone conversations.

"Would you come out to our corporate headquarters and make a presentation?"

"I'm willing to donate my time for free if you're willing to pay for my airfare," I quickly thought to say.

So there I sat in the St. Louis airport, feeling the glow of making that sale to Monsanto. I thought about how quickly my financial situation had changed; how my compensation was forever going to be based on what I could sell, as opposed to what was sold for me; how I now had two clients who were all mine to sell and serve; and how it could all change tomorrow.

I thought about how a professional athlete never knows when his career as a high-earning player will end, and that is how I felt. I would work hard but save as much as I could; after all, this dream could end quickly.

I realized that I was going to succeed or fail as a consultant on my own, with no guarantees, based on what I could sell, do, serve, and maintain. That familiar feeling of scary and exhilarating came—one I was beginning to realize I needed. And I was beginning to realize that I needed tension and pace to help overcome boredom, which often produced a lack of focus.

It has taken me a long time to understand that boredom, restlessness, and a lack of pace, combined with opportunity and other elements of my MAP can be a dangerous cocktail if I don't manage it well. But it can also be a tremendous trigger for success, satisfaction, and a sense of meaning and purpose—at least it has been for me.

For Reflection and Discussion

1. When you engage in work that fits your MAP, it will be easier to realize the purpose of your life and your intended destiny. However, not all items in your MAP have equal value. Prioritizing and knowing what is critical to your success is important, as is managing those critical elements. What are the critical elements of your MAP?

2. How have you taken advantage of and pursued opportunities that fit with the most critical elements of your MAP?

CHAPTER 10

Avoid Self-Destruction

The story in this chapter illustrates that when your MAP—your nature—is not understood and managed well, it can lead to self-destructive behavior that can have very negative consequences. Do you think there are aspects of your MAP that can result in self-destructive behavior? Have you ever behaved in a self-destructive manner? I have.

Sometimes self-destructive behavior is a detour, sometimes a life-learning or life-changing experience, but sometimes it has a more permanent outcome, one that might be impossible to correct.

The summer before my senior year in college, a high school friend came to visit. He gave me a pill, saying, "This is good stuff." It was probably LSD, but I didn't know for sure.

After he left, I swallowed the pill. It was something to try, to explore. The next twenty-four hours were a disaster as paranoia and fear took over my mind, imagination, and actions. I fled, people found me; I cowered, people held me; I walked, people joined me; I ran, people caught up and slowed me down. People stayed with me until they thought I was safe to be left alone.

When it was over, it didn't end. At night, when the room was dark and I was trying to sleep, I imagined evil. My heartbeat would race, even after turning on the light—which I did most nights.

No one knew. Generalized fear and panic fed into my existing fragility. I wondered what my life would be like, wondered if I would ever get back to normal. I was thinking the worst.

I would go about the day fighting myself, my mind, my emotions, and my anxiety. Slowly, over several years, it diminished, like it had to take a planned route and make an eventual exit—moving from intense to dull to gone.

Even after I married Diane, I would lie next to her in bed, lights out, in the darkness, feeling that her presence and goodness would protect me.

Fear like this distracts. It can split the mind; it can absorb focus and energy —like a black hole, as it distracts.

As the fear from that 1971 LSD trip (or whatever drug it actually was) remained in my body, refusing to let go of its hold on my mind and on the way it was making my struggles as a student even more difficult, I wanted to quit and run, to hide, to whatever.

My father took notice and would call, asking "What's wrong?" I never told him. I never told anyone. I was too afraid to tell him, too afraid to continue, too afraid to quit, too afraid to admit, and too afraid to ask for help. I was frozen like a deer in the road, staring at the headlights, and scared that this condition, which I had brought on myself, was permanent.

I had not yet learned how self-destructive my nature could be—this desire I had for experimentation; exploration; dealing with some unknown; and a need for action, pace, and intensity. I had not yet learned how to understand and manage my MAP and to use it as God intended.

Self-destructive behavior can take many forms. For example, one person said after receiving his MAP, "I am built to organize, and if I have nothing to organize, I let myself get disorganized (in destructive ways) so I have something to organize." He described it as "a game of daring myself to go to the edge of total disorganization, just so I can restore myself." Another person, whose Central Motivational Theme is to combat and prevail, learned the hard way how destructive his nature can be. He described how he continually fought and prevailed over people and, in the process, destroyed most of the relationships in his life. The key, he realized, was learning how to prevail over himself, when necessary.

For Reflection and Discussion

1. In what ways has your MAP—your nature— led you to behave in a self-destructive manner?

2. In what ways could your MAP—your nature—lead you to self-destructive behavior if you do not understand and manage it well?

CHAPTER 11

Face Realities about Yourself

Confronting yourself is not pleasant, and change is not easy—particularly when it first comes from outside you, forcing you to face a reality about yourself.

I've come to understand that none of us are immune; we all have something that blocks the potential and promise we have been given. You can go through life trying to avoid and ignore, or you can listen to the words of others and the inner voice each of us have been given. If you don't listen, it can hold you back, preventing you from becoming who you were designed to be—hold you back from realizing the purpose of your life and fulfilling your intended destiny.

This next story you are about to read continues the theme about the importance of understanding and managing your MAP—your nature. How your giftedness can be an asset or a liability, depending on how well you manage it.

At age twelve, I inherited a *Newsday* newspaper route from my brother, Gene. I scavenged an old baby carriage and used it to tote the newspapers, which I delivered to about seventy-five customers each weekday afternoon when I returned from school and on weekend mornings. I enjoyed earning money, but I didn't like the obligation of having an everyday responsibility —particularly one that consumed so much time. After several months, I quit the job.

A few weeks before I had begun delivering the newspapers, I hurt my neck and was hospitalized. When I arrived home, my oldest brother, Jay, was there with a dog he had purchased for me.

This dog, Skippy, was the ugliest yet cutest one-year-old mutt you could imagine. He was a bit over one foot tall, thin as a rail, mostly black with some white wiry, curly fur. He was a true American-melting-pot dog, with terrier being the only noticeable ingredient.

In my mind was a Lassie-type image—Skippy walking with me as I went about my day—boy and dog, free as birds.

Skippy became my best friend. I rubbed his belly and behind his ears, which he loved. We wrestled, ran, chased each other, and played fetch. He licked my various cuts and slept with me each night, and I talked to him—all the time. He always listened intently, communicating empathy and understanding with his brown eyes and floppy ears.

Skippy and I would deliver newspapers together. At first, I tied his leash to the baby carriage, but I quickly realized that wasn't a very good idea when he took off, slowly dragging the carriage behind him. Besides, I wanted Skippy to walk freely with me. That was the image I had in my mind.

Skippy needed to be trained, and I had a plan that I executed well. I piled a bunch of tennis balls into the baby carriage, and at what felt like the right moment, I unleashed Skippy. He ran. I yelled "Skippy come!" and then threw a tennis ball that hit him in his rear. He stopped, momentarily looked at me, and then began running again. I picked up another tennis ball, yelled "Skippy, come!" and threw the ball—another bullseye strike. He came back.

Two pitches, and Skippy was trained to return to me when I called his name. But it worked only when I was within his sight. If he could sneak away and scurry around a house or bush and couldn't see me, he took off—sometimes for days—often returning hungry, muddy, even more scraggly, and occasionally injured. Skippy loved his freedom to roam—it was in his blood.

When my mother got a job in a nursing home, one block from the beach in Far Rockaway, my dad would drive her to work, taking Skippy with him. After Mom got out of the car, my dad took Skippy to the beach and let him run freely through the sand and water until he was exhausted. My dad seemed to understand Skippy's need to run freely but also to contain it.

On July 4, 1970, while I was in college, as firecrackers exploded, Skippy bolted through a slowly closing front screen door. Each day my dad looked for Skippy, calling his name. He eventually found him, lying dead in a ditch. My dad didn't tell me about finding Skippy's body for several months.

At first I was sure that Skippy would show up as he always did. Then I thought that his dog tag had fallen off and he was taken in by another family—that one day he would escape and return to me. I also imagined that he had been run over by a car or killed by another dog or animal. I was away at college, though, and sometimes out of sight means out of mind.

Several years later, after Diane and I were married, I came to understand that Skippy's desire to be unleashed to roam and explore is what eventually got him killed. This awareness partly came about through many battles I had with Diane in the earliest years of our marriage that had to do with my wanting few, if any, limits, on my freedom to do, or not do, as I saw fit.

Doing what was responsible when I didn't want to do it wasn't something that came naturally to me. Neither did completing things or being focused, organized, and disciplined in doing so. These were qualities that were part of Diane's nature but not part of mine.

Like Skippy, I wanted to be unleashed to run freely with no organization, structure, discipline, obligation, or responsibility, but I came to realize that could become my downfall, as it was for Skippy.

I realized that allowing my giftedness—my nature—to go unbridled had actually become my leash. It was a self-created trap, defined and dictated by my genes and chemistry, one I needed to control so it wouldn't control me.

I realized that if I didn't change and use the gifts of my nature in a focused, disciplined, and responsible way, and if I didn't contain my desire to be unencumbered, I would remain unfulfilled, not very successful, and perhaps living, or dying, in some ditch.

For Reflection and Discussion

1. In what ways has your MAP—your nature—been a liability?
2. In what ways can your MAP—your nature—become a liability if you do not manage it well?
3. Who confronts you about your nature when it becomes a liability?

CHAPTER 12

Learn to Turn Weakness into Strength

Sometimes natural talent comes wrapped as a weakness, or seemingly so—a flaw you wish you didn't have. This can be painful. It can disrupt and dismay as you try to resist, only to succumb, or as you struggle to understand and accept yourself and your nature.

I can tell you from personal experience that if you have such aspects as part of your giftedness—your nature—(and many of us do in one form or another), you need to embrace and accept how you have been designed and learn to use those elements of your MAP appropriately, as God intended.

You need to learn to manage its downside—to turn what you think is a weakness, a flaw in your design—into a strength. You need to turn it from something you don't like that may be embarrassing, or something you hate, into something you appreciate.

When you do—when you see it as a strength and learn to manage it—you will have a better understanding and appreciation of how you have been designed, and you will gain insight about your giftedness, the purpose of your life, and your intended destiny.

It was nearly 10:00 p.m. when I walked out the door of the newly built New York Marriott Marquis, trying to shake this feeling that invaded my body and mind. The year was 1986. I was thirty-seven years old and on a business trip to conduct several interviews. But I couldn't fall asleep—couldn't remain in my room, even though I had an early-morning interview to conduct.

I needed to get out. I needed to move, to feed an unrelenting restlessness. I turned right on Broadway to 42nd Street. Bright lights were everywhere, as were hookers, drug dealers, all sorts of night people, peep shows, XXX movie theaters, and various eateries. On 8th Avenue, I again turned right—more of the same, only darker, less showy, and seedier. This part of New York City had not yet been cleaned up. Disney had not yet become the tenant that would spark a transformation.

Just past a Latin bar, I turned right onto 46th and back to the hotel. But I didn't go in. I walked the route again and again—over and over, each time venturing a bit farther. Each time, I observed the eyes, faces, bodies, clothing, interactions, and what was happening, my heart filling with excitement and my mind racing with thoughts and questions.

The girls smiled, asking if I wanted a date; the hustlers enticed. I had become a familiar face—a potential customer. Why was I there? What was I looking for? What could they sell me? Why was I tempting myself?

Around midnight, I turned left on 48th instead of right and walked toward 9th Avenue. No longer were people milling about. Sounds faded into a distant murmur. Everything grew much darker. Fear and exhilaration began to cascade through my mind and body, reaching a crescendo as I turned onto 9th Avenue. I wondered why I was venturing so far from safety and was seemingly unable to stop myself. My heart was pounding. My mind was racing. I hesitated, but only for a moment, and continued to walk into an unknown abyss of the city—and myself.

It has taken me a long time to understand, accept, and tame this aspect of my MAP—my nature, this restlessness that needed control, this weakness in my design, this desire I had for experimentation; exploration; dealing with some unknown; and a need for action, pace, and intensity and how it led to taking inappropriate risks.

Whenever I traveled on business, when all my meetings were done, I found it difficult to remain in my hotel room. My restlessness would overwhelm me. If I was in a city, I would walk and walk, around and around, up and down streets, thinking I was nuts to do so. It wasn't a death wish or an invitation to felons. It was the excitement, the unknown, the risk that was attractive, fed by opportunity and my restlessness.

I realized that when my restlessness is not focused or calm, it can lead to risky behavior. I learned that my restless nature can be overwhelming unless I am doing something intense and focused, like playing a competitive sport. Or, as I learned in Steve Mocko's class, being in a position to read the flow with people and to spark, facilitate, and influence. Or when I'm trying to make a sale or provide a service to people. And when I write, or when I'm with Diane. When I am in my zone, my restlessness is focused and productive—when not, it can lead to danger, and it has.

During my high school and college years, hitchhiking became an outlet for my restlessness. There was something about opening a car door and stepping into an unknown situation that was attractive. And at those moments, when I felt that my life was in danger, I was simultaneously scared and exhilarated, as well as intensely stimulated and focused.

I vividly recall hitchhiking a ride from Oswego to Long Island and ending up in the backseat of a car, surrounded by piles of dirty, smelly clothes, driven by a pock-faced driver who continually grinned at me once I was in the car. His German shepherd dog, growling from the front passenger seat, never took his eyes off me. I imagined the worst—strategy and tactics to save my life continually played out in my mind. He let me off at a train station in Brooklyn, unharmed, next to a telephone booth— scared, but exhilarated.

And as a thirteen-year-old, I entered a car not knowing that the driver was a molester. Once in the front seat, he made his move. I jumped out as his hand reached out and the car began moving.

Out of boredom, curiosity, and opportunity, I would experiment with routes and no map. One trip had me ending up under a bridge in front of a group of disheveled men who were shooting drugs into their bodies. I was scared but felt very alert and alive. On another trip, I ended up on a side street in a housing project, late at night, feeling trapped in a maze, as I continually came back to the same spot. Finally, a security guard stopped me with his presence and flashlight.

"What are you doing here?" he demanded to know.

"I'm lost," I explained. "Took a wrong turn off the bridge."

He directed me to the route that brought safety. I can still feel the fear and excitement as I recall the incident.

I realized that these dangerous excursions had to stop. I had to find a solution, an alternative.

My plan: to work intensely and relentlessly, in my hotel room, until I was exhausted, putting off eating until my hunger for food prevailed over my feelings of restlessness and what it might lead me to do, followed by having something engrossing to watch on television, until sleep overcame me.

I also learned to load myself with work and activity, which required me to begin early in the morning and continue until late at night, squeezing in family obligations and sports activity so that the pace remained intense.

Over time, I also became increasingly aware of how my restlessness had a larger impact on me and others. I realized how sometimes I create situations I feel I need but simultaneously resent, like trying to time my driving to meetings with little margin of error—always rushing—always finding one more small thing to do before leaving, or rushing to family and social events, much to Diane's dismay, who is 180 degrees opposite me. She always wants to be early, to live with little or no tension or anxiety, at a relaxed pace. I learned to discipline and control myself.

I realized how I say things—funny, emotional, or instigating, at times annoying—for effect, sometimes without abandon, and at times uncontrollably, raising temperature, and affecting mood but serving to keep me alert. I learned to moderate my comments.

I came to realize and accept that it is not my normal condition, not my normal state of mind, to feel relaxed unless there is something intense for me to grab hold of and focus on, or when I am with Diane, or when I write, and more recently, when I allow myself to feel God's presence. Frequently I feel I want to be some other place, but I also know that if I got to that other place, I would want to be somewhere else.

I hated this about myself. I wished I were different. But once I learned to accept this aspect of my nature, this restlessness (caused by a need for experimentation; exploration; dealing with some unknown; and a need for action, pace, and intensity) began to subside. And once I learned how to manage and control it effectively and to use it productively, I grew to appreciate it. As I did, I began to better understand the purpose of my life, and this has led to more peacefulness about it and within me.

For Reflection and Discussion

1. What are the weaknesses in your MAP—your nature—that you have turned into strengths or that you need to learn how to turn into strengths?

CHAPTER 13

Don't Turn Strength into Weakness

The following story continues illustrating the theme of this section about the importance of managing your giftedness. Just as what appears to be a flaw or weakness in your design can become a strength when you learn to manage it well, an obvious strength can become a weakness if you allow it to become so.

Many years ago, I was asked to help a young man who was referred to me because he had gotten into trouble. He was sent away to a school for troubled youth instead of to jail. He had become a criminal, breaking into homes. Eventually he got caught.

He learned his lesson, he told me. He wanted to make something of his life, he told me. He spent several hours telling me about his achievements—story after story—some from his criminal activity.

His giftedness—his MAP—was clear. He's incredibly gifted in winning people over, influencing them, impacting them, and seeing ways to extract gain from people and situations. He likes to stand out, to amaze, surprise, impress, impact—doing things that are different, unique, and unexpected—but he likes doing so within a setting that has risk.

"You can use your natural talents to accomplish good or bad," I told him.

I also told him, "You can easily *bullshit* me, easily manipulate me and others, convincing us all that you want to straighten out your life, but you will be the one who loses if you do manipulate."

He reassured me that he had learned his lesson. He wanted to use the talents he has been given for good, he said. We discussed potential career paths and logical ways each could be pursued, and he thanked me for my help.

I thought, "He's going to find a way to amaze, surprise, impress, and stand out. I am convinced that success will come his way." Several years later, I learned that he was in jail.

This saddened me. There is a special place in my heart for troubled youth, born from my own experience, making me empathetic but not tolerant.

We have all been designed to be compulsively attracted to certain kinds of situations and areas of interest and to use specific abilities and talents. Doing so can take a positive path or a negative one. Giftedness is like an addiction.

Yes, "addiction" is a negative word, often referring to drugs, gambling, sex, food, and sometimes work, but addictions can be positive—like a need to write, or to coach, to be a good listener, to organize others, seek responsibility, solve problems, or see uniqueness and convert it to products that help. These become positive addictions when used for good and managed well.

But what happens when strengths become weaknesses, like when an organizer overorganizes a professional staff so no one has any flexibility, or a detail-oriented person micromanages his kids so there is no breathing room, or a creative-thinking boss becomes so prolific he dams up the process with more creative ideas than can be processed, or when a person who enjoys analysis can't make timely decisions, or in this young man's case, using criminal activity to fulfill his desire to amaze, surprise, impress and stand out?

Each of us has the potential to turn strengths into weaknesses. To minimize the risk of doing so, start by understanding the implications of your MAP, and then become determined to prevent it from negatively impacting your growth, development, progress, work, and life. This awareness is the first step.

Once you become aware of how your nature—your MAP—can (or has) become a weakness, the second step is to come up with ways to prevent it. Mostly this involves controlling your MAP as opposed to letting it control you. Plain old discipline. Many have found it helpful to write out plans and build support from others. Doing so should enable you to increase your awareness and modify your behavior.

If you understand when your strengths can become weaknesses and take actions to prevent it, you will have a more successful, satisfying, and fulfilling life, and you will make progress toward realizing your purpose and fulfilling your intended destiny.

For Reflection and Discussion

1. Have any of your strengths become weaknesses? If so, which ones?
2. How has this had a negative impact on your life?
3. To what extent have you learned to make corrections to prevent you from turning those strengths into weaknesses again? Are you implementing what you have learned?
4. Have you been a witness to others who have turned a strength into a weakness? What have you learned as a result?

CHAPTER 14

Use Your MAP to Find Fulfillment

In the best-selling book *The Purpose Driven Life*, Rick Warren writes, "Each of us was uniquely designed, or 'shaped,' to do certain things...God made you to be you," not "someone he never intended you to be." Knowing those things, what you have been gifted to do—your MAP—is a key factor to achieving success and satisfaction in your life and work, the purpose of your life, and your intended destiny.

I grew up not being very good at most things, but I was good in sports and playing poker and not much else. This troubled me, raising doubts as to where I might find my place in this world and eventual success. I had not yet been exposed to SIMA (The System for Identifying Motivated Abilities), and I certainly didn't understand the power it has to help people understand their giftedness and how it can be used to manage oneself and others more effectively. I didn't understand how some of the things I enjoyed doing that seemed so inconsequential were actually guideposts to be capitalized on. Here are a few examples.

I enjoyed taking the train from my home on Long Island into New York City and going to 42nd Street to watch people. I liked it when we had a lot of relatives come over for dinner, and I could watch the interactions at the dinner table. I was never part of any one group in high school or college because I liked associating with, and observing, all kinds of people. I was good at poker because I could read people and sense the flow of the game—the same with playing basketball. I got a lot out of my 5'7" height.

I liked listening to people and understanding them. I liked helping people. I loved listening to my father tell stories about his life. My mind always filled itself with observations about what I saw and heard.

As I mentioned earlier, I remember as a kid reading a psychology book called *The Fifty-Minute Hour* from cover to cover, seemingly in one sitting, absolutely absorbed. As far back as I can remember, I was drawn to radio and TV shows in which people told stories and discussed life issues—human psychology—the drama of living.

I became a student counselor in college because people seemed to like telling me things, and I liked listening to what they had to say—and then sharing my thoughts and observations.

I was like many others who were floundering as they struggled to find their place in this world—their path to success, their purpose, their destiny.

In 1976, when Art Miller introduced to me a way to identify the "heart" of a person's giftedness—SIMA, I instinctively moved toward the process. There was something about SIMA and how I could apply it that connected with my inner core. I felt at home, where I was meant to be. Quite honestly, the whole SIMA process came so natural to me that I didn't even think about it at first. I thoroughly enjoyed learning about SIMA and developing expertise in it.

It wonderfully tapped into my giftedness, fit well with my nature, and enabled me to have the kind of impact on people I find inherently satisfying.

I'm still not very good at many things, and this continues to bother me somewhat. I have learned to accept that. But I was blessed to have met Art Miller and to stumble into a company and profession where my giftedness—my natural talents, my MAP—could flourish. I was fortunate enough to have recognized the right opportunity and to have taken advantage of it, and this has made my life more productive, meaningful, and rewarding. As a result, I have come closer to realizing the purpose of my life and intended destiny.

For Reflection and Discussion
1. Are you engaged in work and activity that makes use of your giftedness—your MAP?
2. If not, what can and will you do to use your MAP—your giftedness?

CHAPTER 15

Flourish and Fly Successfully

When I was nine, my father took my hand, walked me to the kitchen window, and pointed to a bird nest in a tree. In it were three baby birds. I had seen the nest and the comings and goings of the mother but had not thought much of it.

He asked if I knew what the mother bird would do one day. To me, it was a bizarre question, for I had no idea what he was really asking me.

"One day," he said, "the mother will push her baby birds from the nest and force them to fly, and that is what good parents do."

I stared at the nest and the baby birds in silence. I grasped the concept and what Dad was saying. I didn't know when he would toss me from our nest and force me to be on my own, but I knew the day would come, and I knew what he was trying to teach me.

I looked at the nest each morning when I awoke, after breakfast, before I left for school, when I returned home from school and home from play, before and after dinner, and before bedtime. When would it happen? How long until that day? How would the mother do it? Where would the three birds fly to? Would they go together as a group or scatter about?

The day arrived. When I got home from school, the baby birds were gone, but one was dead, lying on the ground. It never occurred to me— what if they can't fly?

I walked to the garage, got a shovel, dug a small hole, and buried the dead baby bird.

I've never forgotten this story, often returning to it as I went through what at times was a difficult path to adulthood, wondering if I would ever successfully fly, with my father watching me from a distance, helping me from time to time, protecting me from predators—including myself—as best he could, nudging me to fly on my own—and as a parent, with my own children.

Since 1976, close to five thousand people have shared stories with me about their lives, and I have come to understand that we are not all ready at the same time to spread our wings, rise from the comforts of the nest, and fly successfully. Each of us has different timelines and needs, and although there are things embedded within all people (a commonality that binds us if we seek it out), there is also a unique giftedness, designed within each person, that requires different stimuli to enable us to flourish and fly successfully. But when one's giftedness—his or her MAP—is ignored or not managed well, it often leads to frustration, disappointment, failure, an unfulfilling life, and in some cases to disaster and even death.

Just as it is important to understand your MAP and manage it well, it is important, as parents, to do the same for our children. We can help the growth and development process or hinder it. And it can be very painful to realize, in hindsight, that one has hindered someone he or she loves.

But I have also come to understand and accept (as painful as it is) that some children are not meant to fly at all, ending up broken or buried. And as a parent, dealing with that is either a challenge to one's sanity and soul or a strengthening of the soul.

For Reflection and Discussion

1. What has helped and/or hindered you from flourishing and successfully flying?
2. What could you do to manage yourself and your MAP better so that you can flourish and fly successfully?
3. If you are a parent, what are the natural talents of your children, and how have you helped and/or hindered their ability to flourish and successfully fly?

SECTION 2

You Have Been Designed to Seek God

Just as understanding and effectively managing your MAP—your giftedness, your natural talent—is a key aspect of your design, and thus a critical factor in realizing the purpose of your life and your intended destiny, so is allowing God into your life. When you allow God into your life and allow His presence to grow within you (on an emotional level as well as intellectual one), you will move closer to how you have been designed and thus closer to living with meaning and purpose and closer to fulfilling your intended destiny.

I didn't always feel this way. For a long time, I didn't think or care about God. When I did, I was at best agnostic and, at times, atheistic. But I changed. The benefits of having done so are enormous. The stories in this section describe encounters I had with others that caused me to reexamine the beliefs I had about God.

CHAPTER 16

Recognize Opportunities God Presents to You

Do you believe there is a God? Do you believe you have been designed to seek a relationship with God—to seek out and feel His presence? Do you believe God continually presents you with opportunities that, if taken advantage of, will enable you to better realize your purpose and fulfill your intended destiny? If yes, do you pay attention to the opportunities God keeps presenting to you? Do you listen?

Or do you believe everything is coincidental, or accidental, or a product of luck, or no luck, or purely a result of hard work, or some cosmic science of cause and effect that was set in motion at the beginning of time, or some other theory? Or are you like many people who don't give these types of questions much thought?

I love listening to talk radio—always have, as far back as I can remember. As a kid, I would put my radio under my pillow when I went to sleep at night so my parents couldn't hear it. I would listen to the muffled voices of Long John Neble, Barry Farber—with his silky-smooth voice—and, on occasion, Barry Gray. I would drift off listening to ideas, philosophies, and stories.

When I got to college and had roommates, I continued, convincing each of them it would not bother them. I kept the volume extremely low. Things changed only when I got married.

"No way," Diane said to me.

All my charm, smiles, and persuasion couldn't convince her otherwise. I needed to adjust and give up my addiction to talk radio at night, when going to sleep. Kicking the habit wasn't as easy to do as you might think.

As I approached age thirteen and my bar mitzvah ceremony, I was listening one evening—late at night, of course—to Long John Neble, whose guests included a head of an Orthodox rabbinical association, a head of a Conservative rabbinical association, a head of a Reform rabbinical association, and a Christian minister. My parents were Reform Jews, and therefore I was a Reform Jew.

I had been working with a teacher to learn to read Hebrew from the *Torah*, but all I was capable of doing was memorizing the sounds. We were only weeks away from my bar mitzvah ceremony. Granted, it wasn't a big deal to me. Maybe it should have been, but God and religion weren't a priority. They were barely an afterthought and didn't have much impact on my life. They certainly didn't cause me to think much.

As I listened to the conversation on the radio, the words of the Orthodox rabbi penetrated the wall of my indifference. He said to the other two (Conservative and Reform) rabbis, "You and all of your congregations will go to hell."

Discussion, words, more discussion and words, none of which I can recall, except when Long John Neble asked, "What about the minister and Christians?"

The Orthodox rabbi's answer was, "They won't go to hell because they don't know any better."

Even with my indifference to God and religion, I felt angry and scared. I was a Reform Jew and didn't want to go to hell. That was a scary thought. His words seemed so exclusionary. Because I don't believe and practice the way you do, I'm going to hell? And because someone is not Jewish, he or she doesn't warrant the threat of going to hell?

At that moment, I came to a conclusion: religion and God made no sense, and I was going to complete my bar mitzvah ceremony, but not out of any sense of obligation or spiritual growth. I was going to complete it for two reasons: my father said I had to, and I wanted the money. Relatives and friends gave financial gifts. When the ceremony and celebration were finished, I was $550 richer.

Once my bar mitzvah ceremony was finished and I got the money, I was finished with God and religion forever. Or so I thought.

Yes, I married a woman who is Catholic, attended Catholic elementary and high schools, and prays each day. Yes, we got married in a Catholic church by a priest and selected a passage from the *Torah* to be infused into the marriage ceremony. Yes, I did attend church on occasion with Diane, going through the motions of standing, sitting, and kneeling, but the words were like white background noise as I lost myself in my own observations and thoughts. And yes, I did obtain a job at a Catholic college. But did I have any connection to God and religion? No. None.

I have come to realize that life seems to have a way of presenting situations we feel unprepared for, but handle them we must. This is how I felt later in life when I received a telephone call from a priest who was questioning his career as a man of God and wanted me to help him explore whether he should pursue another vocation. His quandary was causing him great pain, which brought him to my door.

I felt like an odd choice as an advisor for him. He was middle-aged and had been a priest for a long time. I was in my mid-twenties, not well-established, one year into my career counseling profession, and still learning my trade. I also had no training in God, religion, Catholicism, or the Bible, and I was a nonpracticing Jew who had given up on God, religion, belief, and faith.

He had a warm and inviting way about him. The kind of way that quickly draws you in. He was soft-spoken but at the same time very engaging. He spoke of growing up in a very religious family that took pride in his decision to become a priest. As a priest, he worked as a teacher and later in a well-established church. He described being in limbo—between assignments, and asked by his superiors to "address his issues."

He told me how neither teaching nor working as a priest in a church felt right to him, although at moments he felt good about both roles. He described feeling out of sorts, like he didn't belong. But his faith and belief in God were strong. The thought of being a priest and serving God was still something he wanted to continue doing, but he was not sure what kind of work he would do if he remained a priest.

The work he had been doing was not giving him much satisfaction or providing a sense of fulfillment. He could rationalize that it was purposeful and therefore fulfilling, but in his "gut," it didn't feel like a good fit. He thought maybe he shouldn't be a priest. But what else would he—could he —do? He was grasping for a straw to hold onto, but everything seemed to slip through his fingers. That was why he was seeking advice from me.

I employed the SIMA process and asked him to tell me about things he did as a child that he enjoyed doing that he also felt he did well, that brought him satisfaction. He smiled as he went back in time. First he told me about a baseball card collection he developed over many years. He described the joy he got from taking care of the cards, collecting new ones, negotiating for the cards he wanted, learning about the players, admiring the collection, caring for it, and showing it to others, who in turn were impressed.

I asked him to tell me about something else he did in his youth that brought him joy.

He told me about a fish tank he had and the different kinds of fish he purchased with money he earned from a newspaper route. He enjoyed buying the fish and taking care of them. He particularly enjoyed when friends and relatives came to his home and admired his fish tank with all the different kinds of fish in it, and how he would tell them about each one.

I asked him to continue telling me about his life and to continue focusing on telling me about things he enjoyed doing and felt he did well.

He described how, in school, seminary, and as a priest, he enjoyed learning and accumulating knowledge. He described the joy he felt when opportunities arose to show off what he had learned, particularly to people he felt a connection with.

He told me about trips he had planned and gone on, all the different experiences he had, and the satisfaction he received when he shared photos with others, telling them about his vacation experiences. He also described, rather embarrassingly, how he would purchase something small to use as a memory stimulant for each of the vacation trips and how periodically he would take out his collection and look through it.

I listened to his stories about times in his life that had brought him feelings of success and satisfaction. I saw a theme emerge, beginning with his first story, and remaining consistent throughout.

I pointed out to him that he seemed to derive great satisfaction from accumulating and collecting things—tangible things as well as knowledge and experiences—taking care of what he collected, being knowledgeable about what he collected, admiring what he collected, and using his collection to impress people.

His head dropped, followed by silence, as he retreated into his thoughts and emotions. He appeared more despondent than when he had arrived. He reluctantly accepted the pattern I pointed out, but it was very disturbing to him.

"How" he asked, "can a man of God, who has pledged poverty, pledged not to accumulate material things, be a person who wants to accumulate, collect, and own things?"

I had no answer for him.

We spent the rest of the time talking about careers and the types of work he might want to explore that fit with his experience and this *accumulate, collect, own, impress* theme. There wasn't much passion in him for any of the possibilities, partly because he couldn't see himself in a role other than a priest or in a role that seemed to go against the nature of what a priest should be doing.

My last words to him, which I said perhaps in defense or out of desperation, were, "God made you this way, and your job is to figure out what God wants you to do with your life."

It was clear when he left, I had not been able to help him with his quandary. This saddened me, but I quickly moved on and put the meeting out of my mind.

Two years later, he called to tell me of his journey since our discussion. Shortly after our meeting, he was asked to become the pastor of a church that had fallen on hard times. Its membership had dwindled to a few hard-core parishioners. He described how he was energized by building up the church membership. He got people involved, and he used their involvement to get others involved. He displayed his church, what it was accomplishing, and its energized membership to others, who in turn got energized and joined. He now had a thriving church and parish, and he was at the helm.

It was clear to me, and to him, that this was his new baseball card collection. But instead of baseball cards, fish, experiences, or vacation tokens, it was people. He collected people, took care of the people he collected, was knowledgeable about them, displayed the collection of people to others, and felt good as it impressed others and stimulated more membership. He found a way to use the gifts God had given him, even though it seemed like the talents he had been given couldn't possibly fit the life of a priest.

After the call, I felt a glow inside. I had put the meeting with the priest into a distant place, in the back of my mind, not to be visited, because I had felt that I had not been very helpful to him. His call brought the memory back, making me realize I had helped him after all. It made my day.

As I drove home that evening, I thought of how there are many moments when people have an impact on others but are unaware of their impact. I thought of how people's lives are entwined, how we all seem to be aware of tsunamis we cause but less so about what we say and do each day that are like ripples in water affecting flow. I also thought about how I had a positive impact on his life and how good it felt to me.

Ever so slowly, I began to realize that he had as much impact on me as I did on him. If it was his job to figure out what God wanted him to do with his giftedness, it was my job to figure out what God wanted of me. But first I had to come to terms with a certain distain I had about religion and God.

For Reflection and Discussion

1. Describe people and experiences that turned you off, alienated you from God. How did you feel as a result?
2. Assuming there is a God, would He want you to be turned off and perhaps angry or indifferent toward Him?

CHAPTER 17

The Power in Accepting a Larger Purpose

This second story describes another encounter I had that caused me to reexamine my beliefs about God and how that encounter has had an impact on me over an extended period of time.

This story has two parts. The first begins in 1975, when I was twenty-six years old, and took place one year before I met the priest described in the previous story. The second part takes place roughly nine years later.

My first job after graduate school was as director of career planning and placement at Saint Joseph College in West Hartford, Connecticut. Not bad for a person who had done so poorly as a student for most of his school life.

To be working at an all-women's Catholic college did seem a bit odd, given that I was a Jewish boy from Long Island, New York, who agreed to have a bar mitzvah to get money, was not into God or religion, and had a certain disdain for both.

The school was run by the Sisters of Mercy. Many of the faculty members, deans, and administrators were nuns. I had no previous experience with nuns. I had heard stories and seen images that suggested strictness, but I had no fear or prejudice.

While walking the campus, I met Sister Betty Markham, chairperson of the math department. Sister Betty was not your ordinary nun, at least in terms of the stories I had heard about nuns. The day I met her, she was wearing jeans and sandals instead of a black habit. She was easy going and engaging. Our conversation rambled all over, eventually getting into a philosophical and personal discussion.

I told her how odd and coincidental it seemed that a Jewish boy from Long Island who agreed to have a bar mitzvah to get money and was not particularly religious would end up at an all-women's Catholic college.

I didn't speak of the disdain I felt toward religion, and by association, toward God. Nor did I share what, at best, were agnostic beliefs that bordered on atheism.

Sometimes someone says something that sticks, something that grabs hold and won't let go. Maybe it's the words, maybe the timing, maybe our receptivity; maybe it's all those factors. And that was the case here.

"Always remember," she said, "nothing in life is coincidental—everything has a reason."

Really? Does everything really have a reason? Are there no real coincidences—none at all? Is there always a larger purpose, any purpose?

Her words kept coming back to me, in situation after situation, as I searched for the reason and larger purpose for what I experienced and saw. Understanding often eluded me, and sometimes it took years for me to see and to grasp the connections—if this didn't happen, then that wouldn't have happened, and if that didn't happen, then...

When I looked for reason and purpose from an immediacy perspective, I rarely, if ever, saw the broader understanding. It was like I was standing next to a train track and watching a train go by. All I saw was one car in front of me. But I thought that if I could be in the sky, my view would change because I would see the beginning and end of the train and have a sense of where the train was heading. And if my view was even broader, like going forward in time, I could see where the train would end up. With a broader understanding, I might react differently to situations.

At first, this searching for reason and purpose was a clumsy intellectual exercise whereby I forced myself to step out of my emotions and biases, as best I could, when faced with difficult or disturbing situations.

Like a seed that needs time to root itself and produce growth, the intellectual exercise evolved into an unshakable foundational belief and faith that there is something larger at play in each of our lives, that we are all riding a river that tries to take us where we are naturally meant to go, that we should seek to steer our ships as best we can, but the meandering river will seek its natural course.

I grew to believe that faith doesn't mean I don't try hard to steer where I think I should be headed; it also means I need to listen and learn when the river and ship are not going as I would like—to try and understand and accept.

Nine years later, I was counseling an executive who had lost his job and whose spirit was deadened. I could see it on his face and in how he moved. I could hear it in his voice, and see it in how his shoulders slumped, and in how he sank deep into his chair. I could feel the defeat within him.

I had seen many people lose their jobs and land back on their feet, sometimes in areas they had not anticipated and in better jobs. I tried to energize that executive by being encouraging. But nothing I said was getting through. The sadness in his eyes was a window to sadness inside.

Sister Betty's words had served me well during some of the tough times I had experienced. There seemed to be a truth to her words about everything having a "reason and a larger purpose," if only you searched for it, were receptive to it, and sought to understand it. I saw how a closed door could open a new one; how a hardship or painful experience often led to growth, awareness, development, or some unanticipated joy; how positives sometimes emerged from negatives. It was like someone's hand was helping or guiding. And with acceptance came peace of spirit and peace of mind—to a certain degree.

I began to believe strongly that part of my responsibility to myself, and the management of my life, was to recognize this, grow from each encounter, and seek out, as Sister Betty said, "the reason and larger purpose."

On occasion, in my counseling, I had shared this philosophy and belief with others who had lost their jobs, and it always got people to think; to step out of their slump; to become more energized and determined; and to learn, grow, and develop from the experience—to see it as an opportunity presented by God or life itself to evolve as a person.

I shared Sister Betty's words with this person in front of me and illustrated with some of my experiences and those from others who had lost their jobs.

He was in his early fifties but looked much older. The wrinkles were deep and his eyes swollen. He was listening intently. I could see that it was affecting him. A few tears emerged from each eye. He didn't bother wiping them away. He sat up straighter, stronger, and stared at me. This was good; it was working. "Success again," I thought.

He said, "Don't tell me that there is a reason for everything." His voice was strong and full of anger. I had unleashed something. "Eight years ago," he went on to say, "My little girl was killed, murdered by someone. I have searched for the reason and purpose, and there is none, and a day doesn't go by without my missing her, so don't preach to me about there being a reason and purpose for all things."

He stood up and left me sitting there, helpless and embarrassed. He wouldn't return my repeated telephone calls. I never spoke with him again.

Some people, for some reason, are asked to endure much more than most. For some people, their strength, beliefs, and limits are tested to the extreme.

I do believe there is reason and purpose for how our lives unfold. And that belief has helped me grow, develop, and evolve—sometimes from my saddest, darkest, and most painful moments.

Maybe I reconstruct reality or choose to believe—or want to believe. But if I didn't believe, if I didn't keep looking for the reason and purpose, and have faith, I might still be wallowing. For me to believe otherwise would lead to my feeling trapped by pain. But I have not been tested the way this man was.

For Reflection and Discussion

1. Do you believe part of the purpose of your life and your intended destiny is to allow God to be in your life?
2. Do you believe you can realize your purpose and intended destiny if you keep God out of your life?
3. Do you believe God and your faith can help you get through tough, difficult, trying, and challenging times?
4. If belief in God and your faith has not helped you get through tough, difficult, trying, and challenging times, why has that been the case for you?
5. Have you had experiences that have made you feel dead inside about God?

CHAPTER 18

Learn to Listen to That Piece of God Inside You

This third story describes how an innocuous encounter opened a door, through which I walked, that has turned into a major change in my beliefs about God. It continues the theme that God presents us with opportunities to grow closer to Him.

She was a student—responsible, excellent grades, hardworking, very religious, first in her family to attend college, of Italian descent, whose parents had immigrated to America to find a better life.

At the time of our meeting, I was not aware that she was opening a door for me to walk through, that she was facilitating the beginning of a process. And I'm sure she was not aware of it, either. I didn't understand what was going to happen. I met her a few years after my conversations with Sister Betty and the priest. When I met her, God had established a beachhead, but there wasn't much advancement.

She scheduled an appointment to discuss what career direction she should pursue. I could see on her face and in her eyes another concern, a larger one. I inquired. She told me about her younger sister, who was not a good student, not responsible, someone who partied a lot, who got all the attention from her parents, she felt. She resented her sister and was angry with her parents. She was the good one, and her sister was not. She should be receiving the positive attention, not her sister on those rare occasions when her sister did something good.

"Not fair," she said, "like the Parable of the Prodigal Son."

"The what?" I asked.

She told me about the Parable of the Prodigal Son found in the Bible (Luke 15:11–32). The bad son left home and squandered his inheritance, and when he had nothing left, decided to go home. She told me how the father celebrated, making a special dinner, much to the dismay of his other son, who had stayed home and did everything right. She didn't like that parable; it seemed so unfair. I had no answer and just listened sympathetically.

I felt compelled to read the parable. I wanted to understand better. I then decided to read the Bible. I wanted to be a better counselor at the Catholic college, I told Diane. It took me a long time to read it all—a very long time.

I would like to say that the words had a miraculous impact, that I saw the light, that my soul was saved. It was not like that. But things began to happen. "Weird," I said to myself. It was as if something got inside me— nothing crazy; no visions, no voices—but I did feel something different.

On the rare occasions I went to church, to be a supportive husband to Diane, instead of becoming lost in my own thoughts and observations and zoning out as to what was being said and the happenings, I found myself in sort of a trance, listening intently, staring at the portrait of Jesus, feeling something—something new that I was not familiar with—a beckoning of sorts. It was both intriguing and disturbing. I also found myself wondering if there was really a God. It was a simple question that wouldn't let go. It was a question I had not seriously asked myself since my bar mitzvah.

One concept kept returning to me, over and over, emerging from the New Testament: that there is a piece of God inside all of us, including me. I sought opinions, many opinions. Some people told me that it is God talking to me and that I should listen and pay attention. I didn't want to. I wanted to go back to what I believed and had concluded, but there was a disturbance to my worldview, and I couldn't ignore it.

I found myself listening to religious programming on television, catching myself, changing the channel to something else, drifting back, always listening intently, feeding that feeling, hearing good messages, as well as what seemed to me word twisting, concept bending, self-serving distortions.

I was trying as best I could to ignore the feeling, and then the revelation came—my revelation, not the biblical Revelation.

One day, I was watching a rerun of a *Star Trek* episode. I wasn't one to watch *Star Trek* reruns, but it came onto the channel I was watching. I saw enough to want to see more. Some alien—a Tribble—had invaded the spaceship, and Kirk was doing his usual heroics. The Tribble fed off anger, growing larger and stronger. In the end, Kirk had all the people on the ship laughing to shrink the Tribble. As the laughter grew, the Tribble shrunk, but the Tribble was never fully extinguished.

I suddenly realized that if we listen and pay attention, and try to live in a good and caring way, the little piece of God that is inside us grows, and no matter what we do, no matter how bad we are, it doesn't disappear. It might be ignored, yes, and buried yes, but disappear—no. It is part of our design.

Rather than ignore the feeling of God's presence, I embraced it, listened to it, and it has grown. It's nowhere near what I would like it to be, but it is growing in the right direction, and I am becoming a better listener to that piece of God that is inside me. This has led me down a path I would not have anticipated, given where I started.

I found that when I allowed God to draw me in, that when I accepted God into my life, I also gained a better understanding of my life's purpose and intended destiny. One key aspect is that I have been given natural talents—giftedness—a motivational pattern to be used to its fullest, to do good. The second key aspect is to allow God into my life.

As I began to believe that my life was part of a larger design—God's design—it became easier for me to understand that I (as well as all people) have meaning and purpose built in.

As my faith continued to grow, so did my understanding of myself and my ability to accept the good and bad of my nature—my giftedness—as well as the destructive things I had done in the past.

As I accepted, I grew more confident in letting my life develop naturally. I saw that when I have faith, there is comfort in knowing that I am not alone, that there is power in feeling that I am connected to something larger than myself.

To me, faith is believing in something that can't really be proven, but you believe it nevertheless. My faith, my belief in God, has become, over many years, unwavering, growing within, from a combination of feeling a presence and logic. And with it, peace of spirit and mind settled into my heart.

Over the years, I have read about many religions: Hinduism, Buddhism, Taoism, Baha'ism, Islam, Christianity, and many books, including *The Bible; The Qur'an; Mere Christianity; Conversations with God; Golfing with God; The Purpose Driven Life; The Language of God: A Scientist Presents Evidence for Belief; Proof of Heaven: A Neurosurgeon's Journey into the Afterlife; The*

Reason for God: Belief in an Age of Skepticism; Islam: A Short History; Basic Christianity; Eastern Religions; Buddhism Plain and Simple: The Practice of Being Aware, Right Now, Every Day; Muhammad: A Biography of the Prophet; and *The Good Book.*

I have engaged in many conversations about God and have contemplated various ideas and philosophies.

To think that God is not real, that somehow the *big bang* happened by accident and that we grew from single-cell prokaryotes, is much less believable to me than some form of divine intervention. The complexity of people, life, and all that exists in the universe just couldn't have happened by chance. Maybe God uses genetic, biological, and natural systems. Maybe He created them.

Divine intervention and science are not mutually exclusive. They can work hand in hand. Maybe that single cell grew to a recognizable human form, or an ape, and maybe creation or the human spirit was blown in. These are all interesting possibilities to ponder.

No one can prove the existence of God, nor can they prove that God doesn't exist. This was the standoff I had in a conversation a few years ago with an atheist. My belief is that God is real. His belief is that God is not real. If someone feels there is no evidence of God, he or she could always choose to be an agnostic. "To be an atheist," I said, "takes as much and probably more faith."

I have come to believe that it is important to listen, as best I can, to that tiny piece of God that is inside me—and inside everyone—and to nurture it and help it grow.

Sometimes journeys begin with innocuous encounters and the tiniest of steps.

For Reflection and Discussion

1. Why do you, or don't you, believe in God?
2. Do you feel connected to God? If not, why not?
3. Do you believe that part of your design is to seek a strong relationship with God?
4. Have you been listening to that piece of God that is inside you? Have you allowed it to grow? If not, why not?

CHAPTER 19

An Evolving Soul

The encounter described in this story took place shortly after I turned age fifty. It resulted in an awareness that became the cornerstone belief that this book is built on.

I was standing in a long line at a Subway sandwich shop looking at the menu board and trying to decide between the meatball—my favorite—and the turkey—better for the waistline. I was thinking of the frustrations of the morning: a backlog of calls to be made that I was avoiding; an important document I couldn't find and how I spent an hour looking for it with no success, which drove home my own sense of stupidity; and inconvenient interruptions from people who wanted to speak with me. I was annoyed, tired, and hungry. I needed a good sandwich to escape and soothe my angry and frustrated soul.

In front of me was a tall woman, well-dressed in a business suit, her hair twirled up, and heels and earrings to match her attire. The line was long, so I had a lot of time to think.

She ordered. My turn—the meatball sandwich won out, as it always does. As I started to place my order, the woman turned, and I was looking at the ugliest face I had ever seen.

I stopped speaking and instinctively turned my head away, only for a brief moment. She must have seen me do so. I was embarrassed by my action. When I turned back, she was again facing forward, and with food in hand was gone. I paid my bill, received my food, and also left, hungry but disturbed—at myself, at the world, at God.

"How," I thought, "could God create such an ugly person?" How horrible for her to go through life with the blotches, pimples, and feature distortions she had. I pitied her, felt bad for her, and felt bad for my moment of weakness and how my turning away must have felt to her. But she must be used to it, I rationalized—people reacting to her appearance as I did. But does one ever get used to such things?

I thought of God and how cruel it was to cause such pain for this person and about how pain and ugliness abounds in this world for innocent people. My mind began to swirl. Like fleeting moments in a movie, I thought of events in the news: a mother who threw her baby out a window; a father who killed his family; a despot who killed thousands of his people; a pit bull who ripped apart a small child; kidnappings, muggings, and the brutal beating and rape of a woman jogging in Central Park; hundreds killed in an airplane crash and more dying at the hands of terrorists with bombs; the pain for millions from Alzheimer's, Parkinson's, muscular dystrophy; the devastation from tornadoes, tsunamis, earthquakes, and raging fires destroying homes and all possessions; the obscenely rich living lavishly while others search all day for a bite to eat and a drop of water to drink; religious groups who worship God while killing each other; flies swarming around emaciated babies; an innocent person spending fifteen years in jail for a crime he didn't commit; acid thrown into a woman's face; a brick dropped from an overpass that goes through a car window, causing an accident, and someone is paralyzed for life; a parent who locks his kid in a closet-sized room; and yesterday, as I was editing, I heard about a six-year-old boy sucked into a wood chipper as his siblings and father watched in horror. "Is there really justice or fairness?" I thought.

How could some people have so much and some have so little? How could some live seemingly charmed lives and others become magnets to hardship? How could some be born with such beauty and others with disease, deformity, and physical ugliness? I thought about death, war, and the sickness that some have to live with daily. How lives can turn on a dime. Today the sun shines, but tomorrow may bring tragedy that forever changes us, bringing darkness and despair. How unfair and wrong it seemed. How could God allow all of this, any of this?

Then I thought of the woman who, despite her ugliness and physical repulsion, was working and ordering her food in a sandwich shop. Would I have been able to do so? Would I have shrunk or hidden myself away if I had to live with the physical ugliness she had? My admiration for her grew.

Then back to God—why?

Maybe each of us has challenges of the soul we have to face. This time born with beauty, but it is flaunted; next time born to ugliness, but because of it, one withdraws from the world, the test is not passed, the soul does not mature. Then born beautiful, and it is used to perform good deeds; or born to ugliness, but it doesn't defeat the soul, the test is passed, the soul develops. This time rich—what do I do with the wealth? Next time poor—how do I handle it? Children who are good and children who are bad; work that is fulfilling and work that is horrible; born into a country of freedom or one of abuse and terror; this time healthy, next time sick; this time tremendous pain, next time little pain; parents who love, guide, and nurture or those who ignore, or worse, torture.

I wondered if maybe God created the universe, us, and challenges to each of our souls that we all need to pass. Maybe death, destruction, and pain that are all around us and seem so unfair—especially when *good* people take the hit—happen so that souls can face the challenges that need to be faced. I thought, "This explains why there is so much pain, suffering, and injustice throughout the world. It is for us to develop—challenges our souls need to pass to evolve—to move on."

All this was cascading through my mind in a brief moment, the way no computer can yet emulate.

Regardless of whether there is one life here on earth, or that we are reborn to many lives, or if you believe there is evil in this world or not, I realized that by my actions, I had a very long road to travel to get myself and my soul to where they should be. I realized that this is the purpose of life, the intended destiny that God wants for each of us.

God can speak to you in strange places, unexpectedly, even in a Subway sandwich shop, sometimes in an unconventional manner, using His direct line, His direct connection, no translator, no intermediary.

On the way back to my office, I stopped at a service station to fill the gas tank in my car. There she was, on the other side of the pump, filling the gas tank in her car. I stared in disbelief. She smiled at me and said, "Hello." I didn't turn away this time; I smiled back and said, "Hello." I felt like I had made a small step in the right direction.

I stood there, as the gas moved through the hose into my car, thinking how each day there are opportunities for awareness, realization, and lessons from living that can help us evolve—help our souls evolve—hopefully for the better. Messages from God, if your faith is inclined that way, that enable each of us to become better human beings—better reflections of God's intention and design.

I thought about how the word *soul* means different things to people, but for me, how it means the core or essence of who one is: spiritually, emotionally, and morally, and also the giftedness God has given each of us, which, when used appropriately, enables the soul to become more of what it is supposed to be—designed to be.

As I returned the gas hose and the gas cap to their proper places, I thought about how souls seem to be born to people, and their purpose is to evolve to a better and more complete state—to what they are meant to be— designed to be.

As I drove back to the office, I thought how each soul needs to experience hardships as well as joys to get it to evolve, develop, and mature; how what we think, feel, and behave are all reflections of our souls, as they are, and how they strive to be; and how, in my mind, there is little distinction between my soul and me.

As I pulled into the parking lot, I thought, "Just as my soul can mature and become better, so can I."

I parked my car, turned off the engine, and sat for a moment, listening to some minor crackling noise coming from under the hood. I realized that, for a long time, I had been too caught up in running from my past, trying to be successful, and trying to get ahead—so caught up that my awareness and receptivity about God, spirit, and soul had become dull, dwarfed through a lack of use.

As I walked into the office building, I realized that I was on a journey— that my soul was on a journey. It always has been evolving, developing, and maturing, sometimes (maybe often) in spite of myself.

And as I sat down to eat my meatball sandwich, I thought about how God and time have a way of shining a light so that we can see things more clearly.

As minor as it might seem, that chance encounter was a turning point— an awakening of sorts—about the kind of person I had become and the kind of person I wanted to be—a person who lives his life with meaning and purpose, who successfully works to fulfill his design and intended destiny.

For Reflection and Discussion

1. Do you believe that you have a soul that is evolving?

2. Do you believe that the attitudes and beliefs you have and the actions you take affect the development of your soul?

3. Do you believe that God presents opportunities for awareness, realization, and lessons from living that help your soul develop and evolve toward its design?

4. Do you believe that the development of your soul, and striving to fulfill your design and intended destiny, are key ingredients to living a meaningful, purposeful, and successful life?

5. What would you say to God if you got to heaven and He greeted you?

SECTION 3

You Have Been Designed to Express Love and Goodness

Peter Gomes, a theologian and pastor at Harvard University, wrote, "The news is not that we are worse than we think; it is that we are better than we think, and better than we deserve to be. Why? Because at the very bottom of the whole enterprise is the indisputable fact that we are created, made, formed, invented, patented in the image of goodness itself."

In the two previous sections, I wrote about the importance of understanding and successfully managing your nature—your giftedness, your natural talent, your MAP—and about the importance of allowing God to be in your life. I wrote about how using your giftedness appropriately and seeking a relationship with God are two key aspects of your design and how as you grow, develop, and evolve toward your design, you will be evolving your soul and moving closer to realizing the purpose of your life and fulfilling your intended destiny. But there is more to your design.

I have come to believe that the human design includes universal beliefs and behaviors—a sort of homing device embedded inside each of us. And when we listen to and act on those beliefs and behaviors, they provide a source of strength, comfort, and peace of spirit and mind that lead to further development of the soul and a greater chance that our lives will have meaning, purpose, and a feeling of success. At least that has been true for me.

In this section, I identify some of those beliefs and behaviors. The more they become part of your life, the greater the likelihood that you will feel that you have lived a meaningful, purposeful, and successful life—particularly when they are combined with the successful management of your giftedness and the establishment of a relationship with God.

CHAPTER 20

Change for the Better

I begin with the following story because it describes a major shift in the direction of this book. It was as if I was comfortably strolling along, humming a tune, enjoying the sunshine, and then something I couldn't avoid happened—something I had to confront.

In 2007, I returned to the hotel room I was staying in, after midnight, after my fortieth high school reunion ended. I wrote the following that night as a way to sort through my thoughts and feelings:

> I've heard it said that it is never wise to go back, that disappointment awaits, that good memories can rarely be matched, that bad memories can resurface in rawness you'd rather not face. But there was something quite compelling about this fortieth high school reunion that wasn't there in previous ones. Maybe it was the approaching age of sixty and an unconscious sense that this might be the last opportunity to see people who had been very important in my life at one time—a last time to talk, touch, listen, and laugh— sort of a last hurrah. Maybe it was the flood of emails and the feelings of connectedness they generated, particularly from elementary school chums. Maybe it was that old sense of competition and comparison kicking in again after all the years— had it really been left behind? Mine I know never left but had redirected itself elsewhere—all the Five Towns competitiveness had prepared us well for the demands of this world.
>
> Maybe it was all the promotional efforts paying off, or seeing the number of people attending keep increasing, momentum building on itself, and the feeling of not wanting to not be there. Maybe it was some morbid curiosity lurking somewhere deep in the mind's recesses.

Maybe you looked at the list of names. I know I did. Many I recalled, but oddly, I couldn't dredge up an iota of memory about most and only a tidbit here and there about others. The same with faces— some were very vivid and etched in my mind, but for most, no matter what mental gymnastics I exercised, I couldn't extract an image.

On top of this, I was acutely aware that I saw myself a certain way back then and see myself a certain way now, and the two images don't line up well at times. I know that I am not unique to this self-evolution and awareness—it is something we all go through, shedding parts that no longer fit and keeping parts that do. All this produced questions of how wise the trip would actually be. Emailing from a distance was safe. Being physically present might not be.

There was comfort in connecting individually with two of my then-closest friends—Glenn on Friday for some one-on-one hoops, conversation, and dinner, and Scott for lunch on Saturday. How easy it was—no awkwardness, no hesitation. We just picked up where we had left off forty years earlier. The flow felt so good.

What was remarkable about this reunion was the bond that people seemed to have—common ground that transcended past boundaries. People who might not have had much to do with each other back then were connecting. In some ways, we seem to have come full circle.

In kindergarten, where some of us first met, we had no guards up. We were young, naïve, and so open to a new world and others. The announcement about "Don't forget to eat," or something about no one seems to want to eat, was quite revealing. Conversation, connecting, and people were the main course.

As I drove Scott home, we talked about how young we felt. It was like the scene from the end of a movie. But it was also like just another Saturday evening, at age seventeen, without the parents waiting up, because we were past curfew—the party had come to the end, and it was time to drive home. "What are you doing tomorrow? Call me when you get up."

I arrived back at the hotel filled with emotion and admiration for us, as a class, not only for surviving so well in our lives, but also for how we came together on this one evening and went back in time, and how we brought each other along for a great ride.

Uncharacteristically, when I returned home, not thinking of consequences, I took a leap and sent what I had written to all on the email list of all my high school classmates—those who attended and those who did not.

Sending this note to five hundred or so people really was a big leap for me because I was so unsure of myself back then. In some ways, the evening returned me to back then.

Emails poured back, filling my in box: "Beautifully said." "You summed it up." "We didn't get a chance to say anything more than hello, but having read what you wrote, I'm sorry we didn't." "You made me think what I missed by not attending." "Well said, Steve. I never remember you being so articulate." I loved your email!! You are quite the communicator." "Thank you for expressing what I felt." "How beautifully you've expressed many of the feelings that I experienced, too. Thank you for giving it a voice for us to share." "I had so many of the same feelings of anxiety, competition, regret, and excitement that you mentioned."

After being so unsure about attending the reunion and unsure about sharing what I wrote, I was flying high and feeling good about myself. Then I received this email:

I remember your name from high school (one of a handful) but don't remember the specifics. I have traveled down many avenues after graduation to forget my high school years. They were by far the worst years of my life. I have few good memories with regard to my fellow classmates. Some were nice to me and other misfits I was friends with throughout high school. However, seeing your name brought a chill. I'm not sure if you remember me, and that's just fine if you don't; I'm sure I meant nothing to you—just someone you were really mean to...I'm sure a lot of people hated high school, and I know teenagers can be cruel—but that didn't make it any easier for me to get through. It is sort of healing for me to let you know at this time in our lives that whatever you did hurt me, but I'm sure you were just one of the many who didn't accept me.

I learned long ago that life seems to have a way of reminding us how fragile and transitory things can be. How the past can haunt. But we can't undo what we have done. I wrote back:

> I do remember you, and I do recall being quite cruel to you in many ways. And I recall you trying to be friendly with me, which made my behavior even worse. Didn't I even steal some money from you, and my dad made me go to your house to apologize? If you are the person I am thinking of, I am quite sorry. If you are who I think you are, you didn't deserve how I treated you. It must have taken a lot of courage to write what you did, and quite honestly you could have said a lot worse to me. I would ask for your forgiveness on this, but I don't deserve it for what I did to you. I would ask only that you know that it was not you, it was me, and that I hope that in some way, my sadness about what I did, and what I am writing to you, helps.

The response:

> Of course I didn't deserve the way you treated me (*NEVER* thought I did.) By the way, the reason you did it, Steven, was because you could. Your "competitiveness" with your friends and classmates may have prepared you for life, but I'm not sure what helped your character. In high school I was neither smart, attractive on the outside, nor popular. Tolerance of people who did not fit the Five Towns stereotype was not one of the virtues of my classmates. FYI: It didn't take bravery, righteousness, or an act of God to email you; it was just a way to let you know that your actions made (or at least highly contributed to making) my high school years a hell. Wow, I really do feel better.

The emails were working through me, touching nerve endings, and working their way back up. Flee, fight, reflect—what was all this saying about me, the evening, and what I wrote? I responded:

I think that my character was slow to develop, but the potential was there for it to evolve in a more humane and caring manner. And I like to think that it has. The Five Towns was not an easy place for many, even for people who seemed to have it all, or have a lot. I clearly didn't get to know you on the inside, as a person. The reason I treated you in such a nasty manner is not as simple as that I could, although I'm sure that had something to do with it.

It sounds like it was very tough for you for a variety of reasons… One of the people I was speaking with at the reunion told me how he had moved to the Five Towns in ninth grade and how difficult it was. He told me that he had few friends, never fit in, and had a miserable time in high school. He was so uncertain about coming to the reunion. He is someone I just knew by name. I was oblivious as to how difficult it was for him, and clearly it was for you also. I was not cruel to him the way I was to you, but I didn't give him a thought back then, which can also be quite cruel.

No excuses, but there is more to me than you might suspect. I've come to realize that I had a learning disability. I was stuck in classes with the kinds of kids who carved their names on their arms. I hate to use the word "misfit" (and I know you did), but many of the classes I took had academic misfits. And that is how I saw myself. I graduated with a 65 GPA, at the bottom of the class, or close to it. I was unsure of myself in many ways and not very happy at times (although people wouldn't have known it). I smiled a lot and tried to hang out with who I perceived to be the coolest people. I went to two colleges before I figured out a way to stay awake in class and learn. First was an unaccredited school I picked out of the back of a magazine. Second was a community college. Along the way, I was a good listener (actually always have been) and listened to people talk about their lives, problems, issues, insecurities, etc. I began to appreciate all kinds of people, not just the good-looking and popular ones who helped me feel a sense of importance, as false as it may have been.

I know that I don't deserve anything, but I would be honored to learn more about you and how your life has unfolded. I would like to get to know you as a person, forty years later than I should have. I am glad you contacted me. Please feel free to tell me to go to _____ if you want, but I genuinely would like to learn more about you.

There was no interest in letting me get to know this former classmate better; the damage I did, I suspect, was too great. There was no reprieve for me. I was left with rawness about myself that I couldn't walk away from, couldn't hide in the back of my mind, and couldn't ignore through activity and busyness.

I had been flying high because of what I had written and all the positive emails sent to me in response. Then this laser-like missile brought me back to Earth and shot me down, back to reality.

Who was I? How have I evolved? Why did I change? What changed me?

This book then became more than a collection of stories; it became a vehicle for exploration and answers.

For Reflection and Discussion

1 Which of your beliefs and behaviors bring out the best in you?
2 Which of your beliefs and behaviors bring out the worst in you?
3 How have you changed for the better or the worse?

CHAPTER 21

Unconditional Love

Love, I have come to realize, is complicated. When my father would yell at me or punish me, he would almost always say, "If I didn't love you, I wouldn't care." Those words bothered me back then, but as I matured, got married, had children, and then grandchildren, I began to better understand and appreciate what he was communicating to me. His love for me was unconditional and intoxicating. It is everlasting and, as Dr. Martin Luther King once said, "the most durable power in the world." But love can sometimes come with a price: feelings of anger, resentment, frustration, and disappointment, as the following story indicates.

The more you can express unconditional love to people, the closer you will you come to how you have been designed. As a result, you will increase your chances of living with meaning and purpose and realizing your intended destiny.

As a small child, I would toddle along with my dad each Sunday as he did work in the yard. I was his little helper, pulling weeds, using my toy shovel to move dirt, picking up twigs. Whatever was asked of me, I proudly did. My dad loved having me there as his helper, and I equally loved being there and working—if you could call it that—beside him. It was a wonderful feeling.

I don't recall the day that being his little helper turned to "Do I have to?" It became work I didn't want to do but had to do. The loving aura that had existed was replaced by the darkness of my resentment. He asked, I complained. He insisted, I capitulated.

I always did the work that was required of me, whether it was mowing the lawn, sweeping up grass clippings, pulling weeds, raking leaves or removing them from drains, cleaning windows with Windex, or helping him hang storm windows in the late fall and removing them in the spring. He always said, "Good job." I mostly mumbled and grunted, displaying displeasure and annoyance with the entire obligation and arrangement through words and body language. I would depart as soon as I completed my assigned chores.

The relationship went from not being able to get enough of Dad to my not wanting to spend time with him. Tension became unbearable and the yelling frequent. He yelled at me for things I did or didn't do and for trouble I continually got myself into. I stole things I should not have, like candy from a store, money from a girl's purse, and emblems I pried loose from cars. I caused damage, like setting a fire in a wooded lot and throwing rocks through newly installed windows of homes that were being built. School was a disaster, with each report card producing mostly Ds and Fs. Many nights, my mother would say exasperatedly, "Wait until your father gets home!"

As I moved further into my high school years, there was gambling, occasional vandalism, and broken curfews, and in college there were drugs. But what got to Dad the most was my arguing. He had strong opinions and would seemingly not listen to the thoughts of others, particularly mine. He would go on rants, leaving little room for people to say anything, but I would often fight my way in and wage verbal warfare. Sometimes I baited him with a question like "Is China a country?" And when he said yes, I would argue the other side, in such a way that an inferno of anger and frustration grew within him. We got to the point where if he said "black," I would say "white," and if he said "big," I would say "small." It was so bad that when I got married, my wife, Diane, pointed out that I would often begin sentences with the words "You're wrong." When my father and I weren't arguing, I was doing my best to ignore him. A day didn't go by without my tormenting him in some way.

There were moments, though, with my dad, during those tumultuous years, that would break through the barrier, melt the ice, bring the smiles, and release the tension. Moments that were glorious, like when he said, "Steve, grab the gloves." I would run into the house, get his baseball glove and mine, and we would toss the ball—a simple game of playing catch. He was proud of how I could field anything he threw my way, and I was proud to receive his approval. Other such moments were when my oldest brother, Jay, who was married with children, came over for a visit and Dad would say, "Steve, get the cards." We would play three-handed pinochle, complete with teasing and trash talking. Then there were larger family dinners and afterward my dad telling stories, mostly about growing up on the Lower East Side of New York. I never argued with him during those moments and could listen to his storytelling for hours, even though he told the same stories over and over. This I never grew tired of.

My dad died when I was fifty-three years of age, but one of the best decisions I made, or realizations I came to, came in my twenties. I realized that I could spend my life focusing on the anger, resentments, frustrations, disappointments, and the strain in our relationship, or I could instead choose to focus on the things that brought a smile to my face and joy to my heart—the good thoughts and positive memories rather than the bad ones. When I did this, I regained that loving feeling, and our relationship was reborn and much stronger.

I learned to avoid certain topics. And when he went on a rant, I just listened. I didn't take the bait, didn't fall into old habits. I waited the storm out. I wanted the positive, not the negative, and adjusting myself was a small price to pay.

For more than twenty-five years, we spoke at least once a week—father and son. I telephoned, and if I forgot, he'd call me, asking if all was OK. His pride in me was infectious and his approval intoxicating. I had no greater supporter. Few things could beat the feeling I had when I saw my dad's pride in me.

My father never stopped loving and believing in me. He never stopped wanting us to spend time together, even when our relationship was at its worst, even after saying things to each other that caused great pain. As I evolved into adulthood, I wondered why that was so, given how much grief I caused him. It was easier to see him walking away and wiping his hands free of the mess of a son that I was. But he resisted any temptation he may have had to walk away. In doing so, he taught me a lesson, one that has been battle-tested.

He demonstrated an enduring value: If you have a troubled child—a lost soul—you don't walk away; you do what you can, instinctively, lovingly—as he did—to try and correct things, to try and right the course. And this, I have learned, is not easy.

Life has taught me that when you are not successful in finding a way to save your child, it is like being in a free fall, grasping at anything that will slow the descent and stop the downward spiral. How quickly things can spin out of control. How quickly, you ask, did it get to this point?

Life has taught me that when your child takes a self-destructive path, despite your efforts, it is like watching a scene from a movie and seeing something horrendous about to happen, but you feel helpless to stop it. You want to reach through the glass and correct the situation, stop the production, stop the self-destruction.

Life has taught me that when your child needs saving, you just keep plugging away until success arrives. You presume success even though it may not come. You never stop loving and believing in your child, never stop believing that positive change is around the corner.

That is the job of a parent and being a father, as taught to me by my father.

And when a child is saved and his life turns around, there is no greater celebration or feeling. But when he remains trapped and you can't free him, can't extricate him from the mire, mush, and morass, there is an unrelenting weight that never ceases bearing down.

For Reflection and Discussion

1. Do you believe that establishing loving, unconditional relationships, whether they are joyful or fraught with sadness, disappointment, and pain, give your life meaning and purpose, help your soul develop, and move you closer to realizing the purpose of your life and your intended destiny?

2. Have you received unconditional love? If yes, how did it feel, and how was it helpful to you?

3. Have you given unconditional love? If yes, how did it feel? If not, what has stood in the way?

4. Do you believe that anger and resentment can deaden the development of your soul?

5. Do you believe that it is important, sometimes, to adjust yourself to maintain an important loving relationship that is good for your soul?

CHAPTER 22

Provide Love, Support, and Emotional Strength

Do you believe that your life is more meaningful and purposeful when you provide love and support to others and that when you do, you come closer to fulfilling your intended destiny? How about at those moments when your emotions are challenged and you need to dig deep into your core and provide what is needed, despite what you may be feeling inside?

I stood there looking at my father, numb, tears rolling down my face, smiling and telling him I loved him. The blanket was pulled up to his neck. I touched him on his shoulder, on his cheek, like he was sleeping. I wanted to stay and also to leave—what is the protocol? I didn't know what to do, so I just talked to him. Words flooded out. I don't even know what I said.

Maybe I stood there talking to him for an hour or maybe just a minute; I really don't know. It all seemed to happen in slow motion. My senses were so sharp, singularly focused on the moment—on him. The stubble on his face, the off-white color of the blanket, the pattern on the curtain that was pulled around the bed for privacy, the muffled sounds from the hall, the gray chair, photos on the bookshelf, the nebulizer. He was so frail, lying there with the blanket pulled up to his neck.

The night before, I had held his hand; he was fading in and out. His eyes were closed. Suddenly he opened them and made a joke. What a glorious moment. Then he closed them. My mom was there, holding one hand and I the other.

Now he was no more. At that moment, I didn't realize what is meant by the phrase "Someone you love never leaves you and is always in your heart." At that moment, it was all about sadness and loss, and the finality of death. I had to tell my mother that her husband was no more. They were married for seventy-two years.

The nurses had moved my mother into the hallway. She was sitting there, barely able to see, listening to the sounds and people around her. She was not aware that Dad was dead.

I sat next to her, took her hand into mine, stroked her face and hair, and told her that Dad had died. I don't know what I said, and I don't recall her immediate reaction. We sat in silence, and then, instinctively, I knew we had to go to a place that would bring her comfort. My parents had met on the boardwalk, in Rockaway Beach, New York, when Mom was sixteen years of age and Dad was seventeen.

We left the nursing home, and I drove to a nearby beach. Although it was not Rockaway Beach, the setting was perfect. Mom loved the beach—the sand, the water, the smell of salt in the air, and the sounds. She was a nature lover, and despite her limited eyesight, the beach was a welcome assault on her senses. She was in her comfort zone.

As we drove, we talked. At the beach, I put her in the wheelchair, and we walked along the boardwalk and paths and talked. We stopped, looked out at the water, and talked. We had ice cream sodas, and we talked some more. We laughed a lot. We cried. She remembered. We connected—in a deep way. I've had great conversations with my mother in the past, but nothing as incredibly emotional as this.

She told me stories about how she and my dad met and their courtship and young love. Most of what she told me I knew because my father, always the storyteller, loved telling the stories, and as a kid, as well as an adult, I loved listening to him. He was a great storyteller. But she also told me parts of their story that I didn't know, that I was surprised to learn about, like how they secretly got married at City Hall, not telling anyone, because their passion for each other had grown so very strong, and how the rabbi, when he found out, yelled at them both and hit her. She told me how her father—my grandfather—tried to break up their marriage but couldn't.

Drunk with emotion, she opened up about herself and her life. She told me about growing up and being surrounded by loving parents, aunts, uncles, cousins, and friends; about the boys who liked her and wanted to date and marry her; and about the day she met my father on the boardwalk in Rockaway Beach, New York, and how he swept her off her feet.

She described how they first saw each other—each was with a group of friends. She and her friends went into a store. He and his friends waited outside, stretched out on lounge chairs. He was wearing a purple suit with a big, floppy hat. He was, it seemed, as my grandfather would say, a gangster from the Lower East Side of New York. He really wasn't, but to my Old World grandparents, he seemed to be one. And my mother was the much-protected princess.

She told me about his look, how he raised his eyebrows (Cary Grant style), gave her a smile, bolted from the chair, walked beside her, and charmed his way into her heart.

Mom and I got through that day, and I have not been the same since.

As I drove back to the nursing home—in silence, exhausted—and as I wheeled my mother to her room, I thought about the day my brother, Jay, and I moved my parents from their condominium to the nursing home and the events that led to that decision.

As my parents got into their late eighties and their bodies deteriorated, they were adjusting as best they could to change. My father had tremendous pain that kept him from sleeping well. He grew weary, bitter, and angry. This was exacerbated when one day he drove to a store and couldn't remember how to get back home. Jay and I decided to take his car away. My father complied. He knew it was no longer safe to drive, but he was unable to take the keys from his own hand.

Each year, he ordered boxes of oranges and grapefruits for his children and grandchildren in the north. Then one year, he grew belligerent at the company when none of the ordered fruit arrived. When I looked at his paperwork, it was for an order he had made several years earlier. I told him that the company apologized and that we all received the fruit.

He began ordering things he didn't need, using a credit card, so we took his credit card away. He didn't like it, but he understood.

I tried to discuss with him what was happening, but he would smile, shrug it off, and make a joke about how he and my mother, together, made one person. He seemed to know what was happening, but he didn't want to discuss his mental demise.

The physical pain was very different. His anguish couldn't be hidden. Getting old and falling apart physically was so very hard for him. He had always been so strong and proud.

As for my mother, her eyesight was almost gone, and all she saw were shadows. Although she was in pain, you would not know it. She rarely complained and almost always wore a smile. She had a special way of looking at the world. Naïve, some people thought, innocent, and like a child. But I knew of her strength. She just chose to look at life, and all that was bad, through loving eyes.

Through it all, from the beginning to the end, they were there for each other—deeply devoted and in love. Although he could barely move, my dad rubbed Mom's feet each night in bed, before she tried to drift off to sleep. She loved having her feet rubbed. And before each meal, they clinked glasses and kissed.

Each day it would take them a long time to get up, walk ever so slowly down the hall to the kitchen to prepare a meal, and to eat. Many times, they ate breakfast in the mid-afternoon. The journey, it seemed, started in the morning.

Medications were taken, and not taken, and sometimes we suspected they took each other's medications, without realizing it.

When Jay and I moved them from their condominium to the nursing home, my father was very agitated. But it was clear to us that he could no longer take care of Mom and himself.

There we were, in the elevator of the nursing home, moving them in— two nurses' aides, Jay, me, and my parents in their wheelchairs. It was a difficult day, especially for my father. This is not what he wanted, but we had no choice. My mother then reached out, took my Dad's hand and said, "Don't worry, Tommy. We'll be OK. We have each other."

I lost it inside right there, in that elevator, at that moment, but no one would know it. I was being strong. So much about life, I have come to realize, is about being strong emotionally at tough moments. This I learned from my parents.

Six weeks later, my father died.

As I drove back to the hotel from the nursing home after my father's death, I replayed the many times I felt anger, disappointment, and love. I kept returning to a moment I had with my father when I was a young boy. It was one of those loving moments between father and son.

There I was, all of ten years old, standing alone in the rain, baseball glove in hand, baseball hat a bit crooked on my head, uniform a bit large for my small frame, looking up at the sky, hoping, believing the rain would stop, that the game would be played.

I walked the half mile from my home to the ballfield in a downpour, and finally the rain was letting up somewhat. I was alone. My parents worked that day, into the evening. I was on my own, as I often was, making decisions, taking actions, using what limited judgment I had.

No one showed up. No coaches, no players, no umpires. I stood there for a long time, near the chain-link fence, close to home plate, knowing that the rain was going to stop and the game would be played.

A car stopped, and a man with an umbrella dashed out, approached, and asked if I needed help. I explained that there was a Little League game that night. He smiled and said, "Son, I don't think so. The game is rained out."

I felt a lump begin to grow in my throat. He asked if I wanted a ride home.

"No," I said. "The rain will stop, and we'll play."

He shook his head, smiled, walked briskly back to his car, and drove off.

Again I was alone, hoping the rain would stop, hoping that others would show up, hoping to play the game. When darkness descended, I realized the truth: no matter how badly I wanted to play, I couldn't will it to happen.

I arrived home, drenched.

My dad was tired from his long work day, as he often was, but not so tired that he didn't see and respond to my sadness. He told me how much he had wanted to be a professional baseball player, how he was hired by a bank so that he could be their pitcher in a league of bank-sponsored baseball teams. I knew the story, had heard it many times, even though I was only ten.

He told me how disappointed he was that he didn't make it to professional baseball and to play for his beloved Yankees, how the bank closed suddenly, overnight, taking his job and dream away, how he found another job as a butcher, and life goes on. And then he hugged me close—telling me that he understood and felt my pain.

I thought of how both his parents died when he was still a teenager and all the disappointments, failure, and pain that seemed to come his way. I thought about how much I loved that he loved me, about how I could always count on him, and how he never gave up on me, was always there for me, and always would be.

My father's love and support didn't take away my struggles, but he did give me strength and an example to emulate.

Through my father's death, I saw a light—a realization of paramount importance. Love and support are eternal and enduring, gifts from God that uplift the spirit, mind, and soul, which, along with acceptance and forgiveness, have the power to change lives.

For Reflection and Discussion

1. Do you believe that your life is more meaningful and purposeful when you provide love and support to others and that when you do so, you are coming closer to fulfilling your intended destiny?

2. Do you believe that being emotionally strong when needed further develops the inner strength that has been embedded into your design and that when you tap into this important aspect of your design and behave appropriately, you strengthen your soul?

CHAPTER 23

A Father's Loving Gift

Out of the ashes of sadness from my father's death, I began thinking about the value of a human life and what gives it meaning and purpose. I thought how despite the ups and downs of a relationship, if love and caring are felt and passed on, then there is development of the soul—the soul of the giver and the soul of the receiver. I thought how important it is to give to others. How when you give, you will experience more meaning and purpose in your life. How the act of giving brings you closer to realizing your intended destiny.

What follows is a guest editorial I wrote that was originally published on January 11, 2003, in the *Hartford Courant*, shortly after my father died, under the title "Reflections of an Unsung Hero."

I sat down with him on December 28th as his 93rd birthday approached, father and son, worlds apart, usually connected by a telephone call once or twice a week, he in Florida, me in Connecticut.

He was born in poverty on New York's Lower East Side in an apartment called a railroad car because it was shaped as one long rectangular box with one room leading to another. I was born on Long Island in a three-bedroom Cape with woods and beach as my playground.

He got married and started a family during the Depression. He worked for a bank and went to college at night. One day, he showed up at work to find the bank had closed. He had no father to help him out—his father had died when he was ten. Nor did he have a mother on whom to lean—she died when he was sixteen.

He found a job as a butcher, taking over a shop from a man who wanted to retire. He stayed in the meat business until he retired at age seventy-four.

He worked that butcher shop seven days a week—closing only to sleep, eat family meals, and play an occasional handball game. He prospered.

During World War II, he volunteered as a medic and drove an ambulance while those with no kids went off to fight. He developed a passion and memory for medical information. He could sit with doctors and talk their language despite having only a high school diploma. When I broke my nose and sliced off part of my finger, he knew what to do.

After the war, he packed his family and moved to California. But California was not New York, and so he returned to a place of familiarity and comfort. He started over, and within a few years owned a small supermarket. Serving customers better than anyone else was as important to him as breathing air. He wore a butcher's apron and always had a pencil in his ear. He again prospered. He built the house I grew up in.

When I was nine, his supermarket burned to the ground on Christmas Eve. I remember the sadness, but not much else. I didn't know the pain he felt. I had baseball, basketball, and football. Was there anything else to life at that age?

He tried to rebuild his business. He kept all his managers on the payroll. He paid all his bills. Integrity and loyalty were important to him. The money ran out. He was forced to work as a butcher for a supermarket chain. Three more times, he opened his own business —working six days and many evenings each week—only to see each fail.

When I turned eighteen, he was forced to sell the house that he had built and move to an apartment. He found a job working for another butcher. I went to college. I worked to help pay my bills, but whenever I needed money, he sent it. I don't know where he got it from because he didn't have much.

He was neither wealthy nor famous, but he was loved and respected. He was an American hero—like many who faced tough times and prevailed with heads held high. I visited him as he lay in death's grip, to tell him how much I wished to be like him in his honor and his strength, and his courage and compassion. His values have been my model, and he has been a vision to emulate. What greater gift can a father give to his son?

Thank you, Dad. May you rest in peace.

The loving spirit my father demonstrated went beyond me and his immediate family. I saw how he helped two young men who worked for him. This I knew because they drove his delivery truck, and I was their helper. They were in their early twenties, from fatherless homes, and worked to help their families survive. They told me how my father would give them extra money and free meat or take a few minutes to listen and provide advice. I felt great anger toward my father back then, so I just listened, giving no response. But I recall it now with tremendous love and respect.

The Central Motivational Theme in my father's MAP is to *be the key person whose contribution solves the problem, meets the need, or makes the difference.* My dad used his giftedness *to contribute and make a difference* in loving ways to help me and others.

When you use your giftedness in loving ways—in ways that help those in need—your life will be more meaningful, and you will come closer to achieving your purpose and intended destiny.

For Reflection and Discussion

1. Do you believe that giving to those you love and helping people in need develops your soul and brings you closer to achieving the purpose of your life and fulfilling your intended destiny?
2. What are you giving to those you love? How are you using your gifts to do so?
3. What are you doing to help people in need? How are you using your gifts to do so?

CHAPTER 24

Spend Time with Those You Love

Life goes by quickly—a feeling most of us experience. Every life journey has its own unique flow. We can't go back in time. We shouldn't regret. But we can learn from the experiences of others and our own. Many times, we eventually wake up and become smarter. If we can look forward, and then back, we might prioritize differently.

As I've gotten older, I've learned how important it is to spend time with people you love; it warms the heart and develops the soul, helping you achieve the purpose of your life and intended destiny. Do you believe this? Are you spending time with people you love? Is this important to you? Are you finding reasons to not do so? Are you letting anger, disappointment, or some other negative emotion get in the way?

Starting at age thirteen, each Saturday my father would wake me up at 6:30 in the morning and force me to get dressed, eat breakfast, and accompany him to his butcher shop, where I would work the entire day. It was not the way I would have preferred to spend my Saturdays as a teenager.

We'd be in the car by 7:15 a.m. and at the store on Old Country Road in Westbury, New York, by 8:00.

I resented giving up my Saturdays and being forced to work. And in the early evening, when all I wanted was to get home to get going on the things I wanted to do, it was even more annoying. I barely talked to him.

My father's business was mostly filling meat orders for people who had freezers in their homes. My job mainly involved wrapping various cuts of meat in freezer paper: steaks, chops, roasts, burgers—production never stopped. My father and his partner, Johnny, could break down hindquarters quickly—cutting, carving, and trimming. Meat didn't come in Cryovac packaging back then.

Once I turned sixteen, I would also accompany the truck drivers on deliveries. They were in their early twenties, not much older than me. I would carry in boxes of frozen meat and use good spatial judgment to fill customers' freezers, leaving little room to spare.

By then, I had obtained my driving learner's permit, and, occasionally, the truck driver I helped would let me drive the van on a side street that had little or no traffic.

Driving was not new to me. I was already pretty good at it and had been for several years. One evening each week, my Aunt Ruth would drive her Plymouth to our house, leave it parked on the street on the side of our house, and go out for the evening with my parents.

My mother had a key to Ruth's car, and I knew where she kept it. After they left, I would take the key, after studying its exact placement so I could return it to its exact location, and borrow my aunt's car. Being behind the wheel of more than two thousand pounds of car was the height of ecstasy to me back then.

Instead of a stick shift, or a lever on the steering column to engage the gears, the Plymouth had buttons to be pressed. They were located on the side dashboard, to the left of the steering wheel.

One evening, after stopping and pressing the button to put the car in reverse, the button jammed. Panic quickly arrived and hit a crescendo when I pressed the *drive* button and it also jammed.

"What do I do? Where do I go? How can I get out of this?" My mind had difficulty focusing. Disorientation ruled the moment. Out of this, a plan emerged. I walked to my friend Glenn's house and sought his help. Together we pushed the car, returning it to its place on the side street. I returned the keys to their exact original location. No one suspected me—a narrow escape.

One Saturday, as I drove home from work with my father, he asked me to deliver a box of meat to the Rifkins. There was a Rifkin family who lived three houses away and another who lived three towns away. I figured he wanted the box to go to the Rifkins who lived three towns away. I chose not to ask my father, choosing to believe what I wanted, and drove the thirty minutes to the Rifkin home. They were surprised to see me standing at their front door with a box of frozen meat.

The Rifkins telephoned my father. I could hear and feel my father's anger, which exploded through the telephone receiver when I told him that

I thought he meant the Rifkins who lived three towns away. It took several days for his anger at me to dissipate.

Like a scolded puppy, I barely looked at him, keeping my head down sheepishly, silently listening to his periodic verbal outbursts: "How could you? What is wrong with you? I'll never let you drive again. You can't be trusted."

The table I wrapped the cut meats on was made of steel. On the back of the table was a horizontally positioned roll of freezer paper. Behind me were several butcher-block tables that Johnny and my dad cut meat on. In front of the butcher blocks was a display case. Behind the butcher blocks were a band saw and a long counter. Above the counter, on the wall, was a telephone with a long cord. Sticky fly paper hung from the ceiling. Sawdust covered the floor.

There was a lot of bantering going on between Johnny and my father and the various people who dropped by to say hello or make a purchase. When the telephone rang, my father would answer, cradle the phone to his ear, continue to cut meat and, if needed, pull a pencil from behind his other ear to take an order. He seemed to never stop the cutting and chopping. My imagination often visualized the worst (a finger being sliced off), which never happened.

In the back of the store were two large sinks. One of my jobs was to fill one sink with scalding hot water and clean the knives. Even if I wore rubber gloves, my hands became bright red from the heat.

Each Saturday, liver was cut on the band saw. This meant that all the parts of the band saw would become bloody. I had to clean up the bloody mess, clean the butcher-block tables, and sweep all the sawdust off the floor.

For the day's work, I would be paid $5. This was also my allowance. No work, no allowance. But I really didn't have a choice. It was expected of me. It was my job, and I hated it.

Here it is, more than fifty years later, and I would love to be able to work again with my father, spending time with him, giving up a Saturday.

Sometimes, I have come to understand, we are not ready to learn from what we experience, not ready to appreciate what we have. Just because we are not ready doesn't make the experience less powerful. Experiences seem, at times, to have an existence of their own, a certain timelessness about them, waiting around until we are ready to receive them and all their power.

For Reflection and Discussion

1. Do you believe that spending time with people you love is good for the soul? In what ways have you been wasting those opportunities and focusing too much on things that are far less important?

2. In what ways have you let anger and disappointment or other negative emotions get in the way of spending time with people you love?

CHAPTER 25

Love Never Dies

Have you had moments when you felt the presence of a loved one? When you felt a warmth that was not there previously and you sensed (knew) who it was? That somehow there was a connection, fused by a love that never dies, that lives forever? Are you treating those you love in such a way that you will live in their hearts forever?

I really don't like mowing the lawn, planting, weeding, mulching, trimming, watering, or anything else that involves taking care of the outside of a house and making it all look good. Sure, once I get started, I can work at it doggedly long, and yes, I am proud when it is over and it all looks nice, but it is not a joy for me as it is for some. To me it is a necessary endurance test—one I try to avoid if I can.

I suspected this about myself before we purchased our first home. Shortly after, I realized the truth as I battled weeds, grubs, overgrowth, and the need for maintenance and beautification.

My neighbors and those who drove by might have thought gardening was a hobby or a source of joy for me. It wasn't. It's a chore, but one that gave me great satisfaction.

My father loved to plant things, care for them, and see them grow. As a young child, I would help, but the joy was in the relationship and being together—doing with him rather than the gardening itself. And once I reached my teen years, I hated it all.

After my parents were forced to sell their home, they moved to a small duplex apartment. The owner of the duplex allowed my father to take care of the small backyard. He produced a well-manicured lawn, surrounded by plants and flowers. And when my parents moved to Florida, Dad planted and cared for plants and flowers in front of his condominium unit. It looked so nice that others took notice and commented, and he offered to do the same in front of their condominium units. The condo association didn't have a problem with his improvements or his impeccable maintenance, which he continued to perform until his body gave out.

One day, as my hands were in dirt, planting flowers and spreading mulch—arms, clothes, face, hair, and head dirty from the mulch I had begun spreading early that morning, carted in a wheel barrow from the huge pile that had been delivered and dumped at the back of my driveway —on a ninety-degree humid day—sweaty, thirsty, and feeling tired and angry—I began to feel my father's love and presence. It was overwhelming. This is when gardening changed for me—when it became an opportunity to feel his memory, honor him, and be with him again—at least in spirit. As I did, positive energy flowed, and my attitude changed.

I have come to the realization that something is at play that connects us to those we love and appreciate, if we open up and allow it. By doing so, there is a certain peacefulness and energy that comes and feeds the spirit and soul. Open up; be receptive to it. This, too, is part of your design—part of your intended destiny.

Many years ago, I was counseling a high-level executive who had been fired. My job was to assist him with his transition to a new job. Over time, he opened up about his life. He told me how he had been so dedicated to his career that he lost his wife to divorce and his kids to their disappointment and anger. He told me how the relationship with his siblings was virtually nonexistent and how he felt he had no real friends. And God was not in his heart—never had been.

I thought about how sad it was for him—how each night he went home alone, with no one who expressed love to him, and no one for him to express love. "To live in hearts we leave behind is not to die," poet Thomas Campbell wrote.

For Reflection and Discussion

1. What are you doing to earn the love and appreciation of others—to live in their hearts?

CHAPTER 26

Don't Lose Your Way

Many of us, I have come to understand, develop distorted ways of looking at the world. These views throw us off the path of developing our souls and prevent us from realizing the purpose of our lives and achieving our intended destinies. Confronting these distortions can be sources of change and development if we recognize them for what they are. To do so, we must first recognize the value in the message that is being communicated, as the following story illustrates.

I was eighteen years old when my parents lost their house, the home I was born and raised in. Dad's business failed. His third failed business. Their debt had grown large. Their expenses continually outstripped revenue. I had no clue. I was away in college, about to come home for Thanksgiving, when I was told that they had to move. My dad gave me directions to their new home—how numbing.

Standing in front of the duplex, I stared at the second-floor apartment— the new home— with my bag in hand, feeling awkward. This was not my home. This was a strange place.

I borrowed my father's car and drove to my *real* home. I stopped, looked, drove on, then back again and again, several times, parked and sat, trying to cope, trying to understand, trying to accept. I was devastated. It was only a house, but for some reason it meant so much more.

Maybe it was the comfort, or happy childhood memories, or my own insecurities and resistance to change. Maybe it was the suddenness, perhaps the familiarity.

That devastating feeling never left. Its memory, etched in my nerves, was too powerful. I never wanted to be in that situation again.

I became obsessed with earning enough money to feel safe. And as I grew older, got married, and had kids, *safe* began to mean that if I lost my job and could not work again, I wanted to make sure I had enough money to remain in my home and survive forever, to have enough money to keep my family secure, and to make sure that my kids would never have a similar experience.

I worked long hours—relentlessly—saved, and denied. The bank account grew. I set a savings goal and tracked it each quarter. I cut coupons, searched for deals, played angles, denied, recorded every purchase in a book, monitored usage, and found excuses not to be generous and giving.

Achieving that sense of financial security was like a disease. It became a focus and way of life, but comfort never came.

Many years later, I learned a valuable lesson from a woman who came to me for advice.

She was twenty-one years of age and looking for work. She was referred to me for my counsel. We met. There was something cautious about her. I sensed it right away. I inquired.

She told me how during the previous year, she had her first eye exam and learned that she had an eye condition that limited her vision. She described it as looking out the wrong end of binoculars.

She explained that she had lived most of her life seeing things much smaller than they actually were and seeing with limited peripheral vision. This caused her to develop a way of thinking, believing, and living that protected her from falls, bumps, and bruises. Her vision was improving, but changing the way she looked at life, approached it, and behaved would take time. Her eyes had been opened, and she was doing things to change the way she cautiously approached the world.

As soon as I heard her story, I knew she was there to teach me something. Like other people who came into my life, some as momentarily as she did, there was something she was there to teach me.

Her story became my inspiration as I began the difficult job of adjusting the way I had distorted my views about money and saving. I realized that these views had become a distortion that burrowed in, latched on, wouldn't let go, and caused me to lose my way.

Perception, it is said, is reality. But what happens when perception causes a distorted reality?

For Reflection and Discussion

1. Do you have any distorted ways of looking at the world that have thrown you off the path of developing your soul, preventing you from realizing the purpose of your life, and achieving your intended destiny? If yes, have you been able to release the grip it has on you? Have you been able to use it as a springboard to further develop your soul? If not, what will you do about it?

2. Has the accumulation of money or material possessions come at the expense of being compassionate, giving, and generous?

CHAPTER 27

The Power of Giving

Some people cast a wide empathetic and generous network. Look at the actions of Bill and Melinda Gates and Warren Buffett, who have considerable resources to do so, and the network of millionaires and billionaires who have joined them. Material wealth is not the only criterion. I admire those I have met who go out of their way to give their time and resources. For example, Lynn Rossetto is an executive I interviewed who founded a charity (March Forth Kenya Kids) when she was young and had minimal financial resources. Lynn continues to do this while working full time as an executive with a health company.

I have met many others who give to charities, causes, and people through churches, not-for-profit organizations, and on their own. Some people I've met restrict their giving, while others try to hide or repress their empathy and generosity for a variety of reasons.

When you take actions that are giving, based on empathy, you are behaving, I believe, as God has designed you, even if you limit your empathetic and giving responses severely. When you unwrap your giving nature and let it express itself in words and actions, you become, in part, the person you were designed to be. You give yourself the opportunity to affect the lives of others positively. And the more you think, feel, and behave as you have been designed, the greater the chance you will realize the purpose of your life and your intended destiny.

I've rarely met anyone who does not feel good about the benefit they gain when they give to others. But I had to relearn this lesson.

I had conditioned myself not to be generous with time or money. Yes, I had empathy, but I kept it at bay by staying busy and ignoring or giving just a little to assuage my guilt.

In 2007, at age fifty-eight, my wife, Diane, sought my help. She was volunteering at a food bank and asked if I would assist her by driving around and picking up bags of food that people were donating. I agreed. It didn't take long for me to complete the task. I felt alive and energetic. I felt purposeful. I wanted to do more to help. It unleashed in me a feeling I had forgotten, one I had learned at a young age.

During the summers of 1968 and 1969, I worked as a cabana boy at the upscale El Patio Beach Club in Atlantic Beach on Long Island. The movie, *The Flamingo Kid* starring Matt Dillon, about a cabana boy, was based on El Patio Beach Club. I was lucky to have obtained this lucrative job.

I loved being a cabana boy. After sweeping off the sand that had accumulated during the night and setting up tables, chairs, and coolers, I would head to the snack bar to find out what was made fresh that day and what was not fresh so I could better advise my customers. I tipped a worker in the snack bar weekly to obtain that information.

I also provided weekly tips to others who held key snack-bar positions so that later in the day, the food orders I placed would take priority.

Here's how all that worked: at lunchtime, the lines would be long as people waited for their hamburgers, hot dogs, sandwiches, salads, desserts, and drinks. I would take food orders from people in my cabanas and then walk with my giant, round silver tray to the snack bar, getting as close to the food preparers as I could, and yell out to the key snack-bar workers I had tipped, over the heads and voices of those waiting in line, "Are my ten hamburgers and five hot dogs ready yet? Are my three tuna salads ready, and the one chef salad?" Then I would explain to the people around me, who had been patiently waiting in line and who questioned how I could just go to the head of the long line, that I had "placed my food order earlier" and was now returning to pick it up. I would say it quickly and matter-of-factly while pushing my way to the front of the line, where I proceeded to pile all the food items onto my tray. Most times, there were no incidents.

People in my cabanas quickly learned that I could get them food much more quickly than they could get it themselves, and they grew to depend on the inside information I provided about what was freshly made that day and what was made a day or more earlier. They stopped getting their breakfasts, lunches, and snacks on their own and relied on me—every one of them.

I also tipped the security guard, who sat by the door I needed to enter to obtain cubed ice from the ice machine that was located in the kitchen next to the ballroom where El Patio held catered events. Some in my cabanas preferred the cubed ice instead of the readily available shaved ice. I found a way to get the cubed ice for them.

Many cabana boys did the minimum for their customers, but I didn't. My father had embedded customer service within me, both genetically and by example. And I knew that if I worked hard at taking care of people, they would tip me well. I desperately needed money to help pay for my college education.

One group of women enjoyed playing Mahjong by the ocean. I would carry their tables and chairs through the hot sand to the shore, and about one hour later, I would again tramp through the hot sand to ask if they wanted iced coffees and iced teas, which they always did. And I would carry the iced beverages down to them by the water, along with sodas and ice cream cones (sometimes melting down my arms and hands) for their children. When they were finished, I would clean up the mess and carry all the tables and chairs back to their cabanas.

Whenever someone in one of my cabanas wanted to talk, I would listen. And whenever an isolated child needed some attention, I would provide it if I wasn't running to fulfill food orders.

I became particularly close to a group of families who shared two cabanas—ten families in all, some of whom were friends with each other and some of whom were brothers, sisters, or cousins.

Between those two cabanas and ten families there were thirty-six children, if I recall correctly. Sometimes I would play with some of the kids when work was slow, and sometimes I would listen and engage in conversation with the mothers and occasionally the fathers. The conversations were often breezy and brief, but some were elongated and intense, as they shared thoughts and feelings with me. I did the same. They were my customers, but some felt like much more.

I was earning excellent money that summer but also losing much of it gambling at poker.

Labor Day was the end of the beach-club season and the best tipping day. People often doubled, and sometimes tripled, their normal tips on that day. So if I was responsible for twenty cabanas, I might earn, on a good rain-free Sunday, $200 or more. But on Labor Day, I might earn $400 to $600.

Unfortunately, that Labor Day was very cloudy, and few of my people showed up. This was a major concern. I needed a good financial day to offset my gambling losses so that I could help pay for my college tuition and living expenses.

My dad had his own financial worries—little money and increasing debt. I knew he always came up with whatever amount I needed. He would never let me sink, but I wanted to pay my own way as best I could. I felt that I was failing him and myself.

Only four cabana patrons showed up on that Labor Day, and two left early. All that remained were the ten families with their thirty-six children. They stayed the entire day.

They brought large platters of food. They celebrated, and I watched, worrying about money and angry at my stupidity for allowing myself to lose so much at gambling and for not recognizing what I was doing to myself—always thinking the tide would turn—always thinking that my luck would change. This is a belief that perhaps all of us with gambling problems or other addictions conjure up, tricking ourselves into believing.

Toward the end of the day, I was called over to the two cabanas. All thirty-six kids were in the sand below. They began to sing a tune from the movie *Bye Bye Birdie*: "We love you, Steven, oh yes we do…We love you, Steven, oh yes we do…and when you're not near us, we're blue. Oh Steven, we love you."

I smiled a teary smile—a temporary reprieve from my worries.

When the children finished singing, Mona, one of the young mothers, handed me an envelope and gave me a hug. She asked that I not open the envelope until they all left. When I did, there was $1,000 inside.

I was awed. I just sat there on an empty chaise lounge, staring past the other cabanas, out into the empty beach and ocean, amazed, relieved, and incredibly grateful for their empathy and generosity. I never told them about my situation, but somehow they knew.

For Reflection and Discussion

1. Do you believe that giving to others is part of how God designed you and that when you fulfill that aspect of your design, you have a greater chance of realizing the purpose of your life and fulfilling your intended destiny?

2. Do you believe that when you give a gift to others, whether it is something tangible or your time, your life has more meaning and purpose?
3. How do you feel about yourself when you give to others, freely, lovingly, with no agenda or strings attached?
4. If you have not taken advantage of opportunities to give to others, what has gotten in your way?

CHAPTER 28

Find Ways to Touch the Lives of Others

In 1944, Anne Frank wrote in her diary, "Human greatness does not lie in wealth or power, but in character and goodness. People are just people, and all people have faults and shortcomings, but all of us are born with a basic goodness." What an amazing belief and statement from a young girl who was hiding from Nazi soldiers in a world of ugliness when people were at their worst. Shortly after, she was captured and transferred to a concentration camp, where she died.

Do you believe that you were designed in the image of God, with an inherent goodness and, when you allow that goodness to be expressed, you are developing your soul and coming closer to achieving the purpose of your life and your intended destiny?

There are people who come into our lives whose goodness is a wonder to see. We can learn from them. We are to emulate them as much as we can. They are a reflection of the love and goodness of God, I believe.

You have been designed with goodness inside. Let it flow. Don't let the ugliness of the world or disappointments, frustrations, or anger hold it down. You will be better for it, and you will come closer to the way God designed you to be.

My mother began painting in her late sixties. Diane and I went for a visit. On the wall was a painting by my mother, in a frame made by my father. She became a prolific painter, continuing to do so into her eighties, until loss of eyesight robbed her of the joy. Several of her paintings rest on family walls—two that I cherish deeply now hang proudly on walls in my home, producing emotions each time I pause to look at them and allow their magic to affect me.

My mother's soul is that of an artist and adventurer who loved to touch the lives of people in a positive way, but as a child, I didn't know it. Maybe I should have, but I didn't. I wasn't looking or thinking that way. Mostly I saw her as someone who cooked, cleaned, and took care of her children.

But I did recognize early on that there was something quite unique about my mother. It was the way she looked at the world and engaged people—with pure love and acceptance. Maybe she saw ugliness, but I rarely heard her speak of it, and I never saw her hesitate or turn away from anyone. Her smile and affect could stop a room or turn the ugliest of people and behavior into something positive.

In her late fifties, she took her first paid job, and within a few years she was running the recreational therapy program in a nursing home. She didn't have a college degree or any previous experience, but she had a natural gift.

One day when I was home from college, my dad asked me to take the car and pick my mother up from work. I went inside the nursing home and watched her touch, smile at, and engage people in a way that I will never forget. I saw very old people, slumped in their wheelchairs or beds, staring blankly, gone to wherever one's mind and emotions go, light up as she touched their faces; stroked their arms, hands, or hair; spoke to them; listened; and got them involved. I never viewed my mother the same after that.

Sure, she came across as a bit spacey—sometimes her mind would be present and, at times, you might wonder where she went, but it made her even more open, accepting, lovable, and endearing. Sure, at those moments she often became the focus of humor, but she didn't mind. She had absolutely no airs or pretenses, and if her behavior and roaming mind brought humor and joy to others, that was fine with her. She was, however, self-conscious of how she came across to others, particularly to those who flaunted their wealth, sophistication, position in life, and high intelligence. But I could see that all adored her, bringing them to a place and openness they might not normally occupy.

It was only to my mother that I showed my early attempts at writing—emotional expressions from an elementary school age. Somehow I knew she would understand and accept.

To her, life was always an adventure. As a teen, I had nonmalignant growths on my back that needed to be treated and removed. My parents selected a highly regarded New York City surgeon. My dad drove me into the city for the surgery and treatments, but on this one occasion, Dad couldn't take me, so Mom drove me.

There we were, in the car, at a corner, stuck in traffic. My mom looked left and saw no cars; she turned left, proud of finding a way around the traffic. A moment later, a wall of cars came toward us, surrounding us, horns blaring, accents cursing, fingers and hands going up, as drivers expressed their anger at her driving the wrong way down a one-way street. It seemed like an eternity before the mass of cars slowed to a momentary trickle, allowing my mother to turn the car around. She smiled—to her it was an adventure.

I recall traveling with my parents to take my brother, Gene, to college. On the way home, Dad asked Mom to drive so he could rest in the backseat. I moved to the front. Fifteen minutes later, my dad woke up, yelling to my mother that the speedometer was registering ninety miles per hour. She smiled. To her it was an adventure.

When I was a small child, we would walk up and down streets; she would point to unusually shaped trees that she loved looking at and turn cracks in the sidewalk into various games.

Throughout her life, she and my father traveled, and wherever she went, she collected a rock or a shell. She remembered each one, where she found it, and the moment. She would often lose herself in her thoughts and emotions, and I would wait a few seconds before saying something that would bring her back to the present.

With prompting, she enjoyed telling stories about herself. Mostly they involved family and nature. Her favorite was about being a little girl and how my grandfather held her with outstretched arms on a bluff overlooking the Atlantic Ocean during a hurricane, her face to the wind, saying, "Feel the force and beauty of nature." He wanted her to share his passion, which she did. She never lost that sense of wonderment about the world and the people she met.

One of her paintings I own and cherish is of a winding country road with trees, wispy grass, and mountains in the back. The road she painted was the one she recalled walking on as a small girl who decided to walk to Russia to visit relatives she had heard much about but had not met.

When she was a little girl, she ventured off a road into the woods, against her father's rules, because she heard the flow of water, which she found. She took off her shoes and socks and waded into the stream. It was a passion and behavior she never lost—taking action whenever she heard water or saw a stream, lake, river, or ocean. She just had to take off her shoes and socks and step in.

She described to me how as a young child, she loved dancing as if she were a butterfly and how, at age sixteen, a Broadway producer saw her dance and offered her a job, but her father wouldn't allow it. Her early years were very sheltered, she told me with no bitterness.

There were stories about her mother, father, and aunts and uncles who loved her so dearly—their struggles, histories, and love and support of each other; their hard work and playfulness; their history as Cossacks, engineers, writers, and performers. My dad told many of her stories, but when I was alone with my mother, with prompting from me; she enjoyed telling me her stories and my interest in her life.

As my parents' financial situation grew increasingly worse, my father's explosive temper was set off by things I did, but also by little things my mother did—mostly innocent oversights and mistakes. When anger got into him, he could not easily let go—several days would need to pass. We would all avoid him during these times, but sometimes his angry words were continuous and unmerciful. Sometimes I would play my mother's defender, and the words flew my way.

Just before I entered my senior year of college, I was alone in the car with Dad, and he apologized for all the years of his anger and outbursts at Mom. Whatever hate I had toward him began to disappear. Love and hate, and admiration and disappointment, are really not very far apart, and forgiveness can be wonderfully therapeutic.

In her mid-seventies, my mother taught herself to speak Russian.

"Why?" I asked her.

She was reluctant to tell me, but I persisted, and knowing her well, guessed correctly.

"Yes," she said, "I want to speak in Russian to my relatives when I go to heaven—I am not going to die until I can speak it well enough."

She told me how each night before going to sleep, she would look up to the sky and make up a poetic prayer to God. And in her eighties, she confided in me that she believed that Jesus was the son of God.

Periodically, I would fly to Florida to visit with her in the nursing home.

She always wanted to go someplace—away from the nursing home, often to the beach, and just as frequently for a strawberry milkshake. Sometimes we would just drive around. She never lost her love for adventure and exploration. She never complained and was the easiest person to speak with. You could tell her anything, and she would understand and accept you.

How she touched, loved, and interacted with people came very naturally to my mother, and you could see that almost everyone felt loving and good in her presence.

I recognize that I cannot be her, but I can try to emulate her loving and caring ways.

Then one day, I thought about Jesus and the goodness that poured forth as He spoke to, interacted with, and touched people. I thought about how He, too, was there to be emulated and that when He said, "I am the way," He was also talking about His behavior, His way of interacting with the world, His way of treating people, as being the path, the way.

So when anger came or when self-serving opportunities to take advantage of others arose, or when my initial reaction was to pass on being understanding, accepting, giving, caring, generous, forgiving, and loving, I would ask myself, "What would Jesus think and do?" I began to realize that when I successfully believe and behave as Jesus would, there is a joy and peacefulness I experience, and the more I experience it, the better I feel; the closer I come to being who I was designed to be; and the more purposeful, meaningful, and successful I feel I am being with my life.

When you allow yourself to touch the lives of others positively, you feed your soul. As you do, there is a greater likelihood that your life will have meaning and purpose.

"For it is in giving that we receive," Saint Francis of Assisi wrote.

For Reflection and Discussion

1. Do you believe you were designed in the image of God, with an inherent goodness? Do you believe that when you allow that goodness to be expressed, you are developing your soul and coming closer to achieving the purpose of your life and your intended destiny?

2. How do you go about positively touching the lives of others?
3. How do you feel about yourself when you positively touch the lives of people?
4. When someone reaches out and positively touches your life, how do you feel?

CHAPTER 29

Do Right by People

J. R. R. Tolkien wrote, "Faithless is he who says farewell when the road darkens." Do those words connect with your core? Is doing right by people important to you? Have you stood by people when you should have? Has anyone abandoned you when they should not have? Is loyalty a quality you admire in others? Is it a quality you admire in yourself? When there is a need for you to be loyal, to do right by people, do you rise to the occasion?

It is not always easy to do right by people, to stand with them, to provide support, to be loyal. And many times, there are consequences for doing so, a price to be paid. But there are benefits to you and the development of your soul, even though the immediate consequences may be negative.

Taking the right actions in support of others—doing the right thing—is part of how you have been designed. When you live out this and other important aspects of your design, you will live a more meaningful and purposeful life, and come closer fulfilling your intended destiny.

This is a lesson I learned from my father.

I was expelled from school in kindergarten. Really! It's difficult to believe that I was and a bit embarrassing to admit. But I'm not traumatized by the memory. I'm more intrigued by it and intrigued by the thought that I might be the only kid who was ever kicked out of kindergarten and expelled for a few days.

The act that caused the expulsion took place in the morning, and I had to spend the day in the principal's office—a tiny kid sitting on a big chair, like the Lily Tomlin character Edith Ann, feet dangling, antsy, and fidgety.

My mother didn't have a car, so I had to wait for the school bus to take me home. When I arrived home, my mother was hanging a bathroom curtain. I didn't realize that she would know what I had done. But she did, of course. She yelled at me as any good mother would, chomped her teeth, and angrily said, "How would you like to be bitten?" A bit scary, but I understood.

Here's what happened. Some of us kids were already in the classroom, looking out the window at students who were arriving. Lanny said something nasty about my friend, David, who was crossing the school yard. I defended David by getting into a fight with Lanny, and I bit his leg. I don't remember what was said. I don't remember the fight or the bite. I do remember sitting in the chair in the principal's office and dangling my feet, and my mom hanging the curtain, making the chomping sound, and asking if I would like to be bitten. I don't recall how many days I was banned from school.

It's a bit embarrassing to tell people that I was kicked out of kindergarten for biting another kid on the leg, so I never told anyone about it. I certainly wouldn't condone my behavior, but truth be told, there is a part of this—a small part—that I'm proud of.

I stood up for a friend. I did right by him and paid a price. I agree that there were better paths I could have taken other than fighting and biting. I guess my five-year-old mind took the only course it could see.

Doing right by people has its own reward—emotionally, psychologically —and sometimes leads to significant payoffs. But sometimes it results in a price being paid, and on occasion, it results in a person asking, "Was it really worth it?" Of course I didn't understand any of that back then. I just knew that I had to defend my friend, David. But I learned.

My father did right by his employees, and doing so contributed to his losing a small supermarket he owned. It burned to the ground on a Christmas Eve when I was a young child.

He decided to keep several of his employees on the payroll while he rebuilt, using the insurance money. He worked out financial deals with all his creditors. All agreed. But then one became a shark who bit, drawing blood, causing the other creditors to attack, to get what little flesh was left. Dad never reopened his supermarket and never recovered financially.

Lessons I have come to understand are packaged in many ways—in good experiences, in bad experiences, and from example, disguised or apparent, depending on your view. But they often need time to seep through pores, to meander through the body, to settle in the right place in the mind and heart, to produce their magic.

My father would tell me about a man named Mandal. After my dad's father died, Mandal stepped into the lives of my dad and his mother and siblings, helping out financially and emotionally. Years later, as Mandal aged and could no longer work, my father went to each shop near where Mandal got his food and other things he needed to survive. He said to each shop owner, "Take care of him. Give him what he needs; I will pay his bills." And my dad did, for years, until Mandal died, even though my father didn't have much money for himself and his family.

And when my dad's mother died, his older sister, Anna, who was eighteen years old, married an older man, who took in my dad and his two younger siblings. After my father and his younger siblings were old enough to live on their own, Anna left the man. Anna did what she felt she had to do to keep her family together. When Anna grew so old that she couldn't take care of herself, my father and mother took her in. By then, the house they had built was lost, and my parents were living in a small apartment.

My father paid a financial price for his loyalty, but he received so much more in return—certainly my admiration, even though at the time I was not thinking that way.

This all entered my mind when an opportunity arose to leave People Management, which had grown dependent on me for the large amount of sales revenue I was producing each year.

The offer that was dangled in front of me was lucrative, much better than my current deal. The firm that was soliciting me had a prestigious name and reputation. There was enormous potential to increase my exposure, gain entry into more executive corporate suites at higher levels, and earn an astronomical amount of money. I was being seduced, and my head was spinning.

The owner of People Management, Art Miller, for whom I worked, had given me an opportunity when I was twenty-six years old. I was as green and naïve as you can imagine when he hired me. Art treated me like a son. His own son, Kim, who was also in the business, felt like a brother to me, but he didn't have the natural sales abilities to keep the ship going.

I thought of my father and the loyalty he exemplified. I turned down the offer, stayed, and through hard work and God's grace, the business grew and was successful for many years. Kim and I became business partners, complementing each other well—he was Mr. Inside (handling the technical, financial, administrative, and managerial aspects of the business), and I was Mr. Outside (meeting with prospects and clients to grow the business and servicing what I sold). We trusted and respected each other and merged our natural talents.

Loyalty, I have come to understand, is given and earned, but despite the outcome and price paid, doing right by people has tremendous value on its own.

When you make the right choice, you are, at least for that moment, being more the person you were designed to be.

For Reflection and Discussion

1. Do you believe that doing right by people is good for the development of your soul—moving you closer to realizing the purpose of your life and fulfilling your intended destiny?
2. Have you done right by people? How did you feel about yourself as a result?
3. Have you not done right by people? How did you feel about yourself as a result?
4. How did you feel when someone did right by you?
5. How did you feel when someone didn't do right by you?

CHAPTER 30

Use Tough Love When Needed

Have you successfully overcome an addiction that was physically and mentally difficult? If yes, what was the key to your success? Have you ever kicked a drug habit? Doing so is not easy. For those of you who have walked down this path, you know what I'm referring to. The drug (the addicting dependency) takes control of your body and mind. Once the physical pain is gone, the mental pain remains, sometimes for years, tormenting you and enticing you to seek relief.

The mind doesn't easily let go. It wants what it wants. Determination helps. So does having an image or goal—something tangible to shoot for that trumps and replaces the addiction. Also critical is having someone in your corner who is supportive and strong when you become weak, when doubt sets in, when backsliding is most likely to happen.

As an academic, I took to smoking a pipe. It was part of my image. I owned several kinds of pipes and a rack to place them in. I also owned several lighters, pipe cleaners, and a tin where I stored my tobacco. My tobacco brand of choice was Borkum Riff.

I started smoking cigarettes when I was five years old. I stole them from my parents. By age ten, I was inhaling.

Learning to inhale involved buying a pack of Spring cigarettes—for my parents, I told the shopkeeper. I crouched behind a wall at the elementary school so no one could see me, lighting up, inhaling, coughing, inhaling again, coughing again…and again and again until I had consumed the smoke from several cigarettes. I stood up, and the world spun. I felt nauseated and stumbled about for several minutes as it all took its effect. I was now hooked and a man.

Twenty years later, into my third year of marriage, with graduate school finished, I was starting a new job at Saint Joseph College. I was still a cigarette smoker and now also a pipe tobacco smoker who inhaled.

My wife, Diane, didn't smoke cigarettes, although both her parents did, as did mine. So did seemingly everyone else from that generation, as the hit TV show *Mad Men* so aptly demonstrated.

We were settling into a life of adulthood, and the prospect of having children entered into our conversations. I was excited by the idea.

One night, Diane said, "We won't have any children until you stop smoking." She said it so matter-of-factly that there was no further discussion. It was not a question. It was a statement. A fact I had to deal with.

It worked—my choice: tobacco or kids. Several days later, I placed my pipes, pipe rack, lighters, pipe cleaners, and pouch of Borkum Riff on the top shelf of a closet and finished the last of my Tareyton cigarettes. I was going to do it. I was going to stop smoking.

Within two days, doubt set in. The tobacco contents on the top shelf of the closet were calling out to me. I wavered and retrieved them, but rather than begin smoking again, I placed them on the kitchen table.

I called Diane to come into the room for support and scooped up all the items I had put on the table. With Diane in tow, I walked out our apartment door to the outside, placed the pipes, rack, and all the tobacco items on the sidewalk, and smashed it all with a hammer, into pieces, in front of Diane. What was my real commitment to no longer smoking if the tobacco items remained on the top shelf of the closet, waiting to be used again? What was my real commitment to becoming a father if I didn't destroy all the things I used to engage in smoking, to minimize the temptation?

But that was just the start. I was an addict. I got tremors. I had difficulty concentrating. My gums felt like they were continuously sweating. I was edgy, nervous, and in physical pain. I went to a pharmacy and bought Nicoban. Taking it helped. The physical symptoms and pain diminished. I could function again. Nicoban was my methadone. Three weeks later, I drove from pharmacy to pharmacy looking for Nicoban. I had run out. I was an addict again, this time to Nicoban. I decided to kick my dependency cold turkey.

Overcoming the physical dependence was tough, but it diminished rather quickly. The mental dependency was tougher, lasting for many years. More than ten years later, I was still fighting the urge and still dreaming about smoking.

Two years after quitting, Kevin was born. I didn't hand out cigars. Just short of three years after Kevin's birth, Katie was born. As I held each, I was transported into another world. Happiness. Joy. Excitement. A great adventure began.

In 2008, Katie gave birth to David, our first grandchild.

As I held David and looked into his face and eyes, I was again transported into another world. I couldn't get enough of the moment: the instant love and protective bonding I felt; his bright eyes, delicate nose, and round cheeks; each movement and curl of his mouth and lips; his soft hair, tiny feet, tiny toes, tiny hands, and tiny fingers; his steady breathing, coos, cries, sneezes, and yawns; and the warmth I felt when I held him closely. I couldn't get enough of seeing him snuggle close to my daughter, his mom, for comfort and the beaming of his dad.

Three years later, the same sights and feelings returned with the birth of Libby, my second grandchild.

Fast-forward to the year 2016. David was seven years old, and Libby was four. There I was sitting on the couch watching a football game, with David snuggled in the crook of one arm and Libby snuggled in the other. It gave me pause. Could life be any better?

I thought of how young I was when Kevin and Katie were born—perhaps I was too young, busy, and immature to really appreciate the miracle of life. I don't recall taking it all in as a parent like I did as a grandfather. I thought of my friend, Ralph, jokingly saying to me that if he knew how good grandchildren were, he would have had them first. I thought about how as a parent there is so much to think about, do, and worry about, but as a grandparent, there is mostly the opportunity for pure joy.

I also thought of how, as a kid, I tortured myself learning to inhale cigarette smoke, thinking it was the sign of being a man. I thought about how we all continue to evolve, sometimes in spite of ourselves, and many times because someone, out of love, is willing to invest in us, willing to take a stand, willing to challenge and confront. Love should know no bounds, even tough love. It is our greatest gift to give and to receive, and when we do, we move closer to fulfilling the purpose of our lives and our intended destinies.

For Reflection and Discussion

1. When someone tries to help you become better—to learn, develop, overcome, prevail, and change a behavior or habit—do you accept or resist? Do you make it easy or difficult? Are you welcoming, or are you discouraging and defensive?

CHAPTER 31

Be a Good Example

I've heard professional athletes and famous performers state that they are not anyone's role model and don't want to be. They want to be free to live their lives and do as they please, without the burden of needing to be a good example. They want to be free from that responsibility. And I've seen and heard others embrace that role and responsibility with appreciation and gratitude. Truth is, we are all role models. We are all an example to others, whether for good or for bad, whether we want to be or not.

Do you believe that being a good example to others is part of your design, and when you embrace that part, you will strengthen your soul and give meaning and purpose to your life?

You may pass on opportunities to be a positive example, or you may not even recognize that they are opportunities to do so; however, the more you take advantage of them and embrace the role of being a good example, the closer you will come to fulfilling your intended destiny.

These opportunities can be major—obvious to all who see—or they may emerge from small, everyday occurrences, as the following story illustrates.

Heights and me—not a great combination. We are not meant to be together. Put me high up without a sense of security, like having four walls around me, and my legs get wobbly and the nerves that run from my toes to my groin get called to action, vibrating to accentuate.

I've tried to look over canyon walls, creeping ever so slowly, bending as I got close, leaving my legs and torso three feet behind my head and eyes—my braveness tested. I have ridden up glass-enclosed elevators and gripped the railing, as if that would somehow protect me. I have become weak-kneed when I read stories and saw photos of people on narrow rope bridges that stretch across rivers, or that glass floor the Hualapai Tribe built over a part of the Grand Canyon (Skywalk), where you can look down through the glass floor four thousand feet below, and a similar one built over Niagara Falls.

I'm in awe of window washers standing on scaffolding that dangles from the sides of skyscrapers, painters hanging by ropes from the peaks of bridges, and riveters walking the steel beams that reach for the sky.

This fear was in my mind the first fall after Diane and I purchased our first house. This was Connecticut, and trees were all around. The colors of red, brown, green, and yellow in all their shades and variations were marvelous. But as fall moved toward winter, the leaves fell, and many ended up in the gutters that hung from the roof. They clogged the drains, so water poured over the gutters, drenching the ground and causing seepage into our basement. The solution: clean the leaves from each gutter.

The front of the house was easy. All I had to do was stand on a six-foot ladder, reach up to pull out the leaves and mush, and toss it to the ground below. The back of the house was another matter. The roof and gutter were two stories above. My six-foot ladder would not do.

Ernie lived across the street. He adopted me and my ineptness as a young homeowner. He showed me how to kill grubs that were destroying my lawn, helped me replace a threshold to the front door, and taught me how to weatherstrip. He was in his seventies and was the kind of homeowner who would take out his extension ladder and climb onto his roof to fix shingles or the TV antenna.

Ernie knew about my fear of heights. He encouraged me: "You can do it; it's easy." But it didn't really help when he told me a story about an incident that happened when he was a young man. While he was shingling a roof, he fell, tumbled down the roof, and at the last moment grabbed the gutter—holding on, dangling until help arrived.

I borrowed his extension ladder, carried it across the street, struggled to set it in place, pulled the rope to lift the extension, and let the clamps lock into place. It didn't look that high. "I can do this," I thought.

The first five or six steps up the ladder were not bad. I looked down—hmm! Not sure about this. I proceeded to the top—my eyes were above the gutter. My right hand reached in and grabbed some leaves and mush. I turned to toss it to the ground. As I looked down, leaves fell from my hand, adrenaline rushed and flooded my body. I grabbed the sides of the ladder, and my nerves vibrated from toes to groin—up and down, and up and down. My legs grew wobbly. I was hanging on for my life, frozen, pressed as hard as I could against the ladder.

There were no answers to my calls for help, no miracles to my prayers. How could I have been so stupid to think that I could actually do this— actually climb up this ladder and clean out the gutter? Why didn't I just hire someone, even pay one of the neighborhood kids? I was stranded on the ladder. I had to do something. I couldn't just hang there forever.

Ever so slowly and carefully, I moved down the ladder, making sure both feet were secure on each step, hands clutching it like a vise. As my feet touched ground, I let out a giant sigh. I turned and saw that my three-year-old son, Kevin, was standing there, staring at me.

Kevin was, and still is, very verbal. He never spoke baby talk. At around eighteen months, he started talking in complete sentences.

Staring at me, he said, "What are you doing, Dad?"

"Cleaning leaves from the gutter."

"Are you done?"

"No."

I stood there, feeling inadequate, looking at Kevin, who was looking at me and up at the roof. "I have to be an example to him," I thought. "I have to do this."

I climbed back up that ladder, pulled leaves and mush from one section, climbed down, moved the ladder several feet, climbed back up, pulled out more leaves and mush, up and down, up and down—until the gutter was totally cleaned. My nerves shot up and down my wobbly legs—coming and going and coming back again—until I finished the job.

That evening, as I gave Kevin a bath, read him a story, and put him to bed, I thought, "It's amazing what one can do when he has to do it." I was his father; I had to climb back up. I had to do it for him. I couldn't let my own fear prevent me from doing what I had to do. I had to be an example. I couldn't let him down, and I couldn't let myself down.

That moment is one I am proud of, and there are others, but there are also many moments when my behavior was far from exemplary, when I screamed, yelled, didn't listen, didn't understand. As I changed, I realized how wrong my attitude and behavior were. I vowed to be different, to become a better person, to connect better with the natural goodness that is inside me—inside each of us.

It is difficult to always be a good example, but striving to be so develops the soul, and I work at it every day.

For Reflection and Discussion

1. Do you believe you are given opportunities to be a good example to others and that when you seize those opportunities and become a good example, you strengthen your soul, give meaning and purpose to your life, and move closer to how you have been designed and closer to fulfilling your intended destiny?

2. When you were a good example to someone, how did you feel about yourself?

3. When you were a bad example to someone, how did you feel about yourself?

4. When someone was a good example to you, how did you feel about that person, and how did his or her good example affect your life?

5. When someone was a bad example to you, how did you feel about that person, and how did his or her bad example affect your life?

CHAPTER 32

Stand Up for People Being Treated Unfairly

How do you feel when you see someone being treated unfairly? Is your initial instinct to take action? I suspect that even when you are the person who is taking the unfair action, there seems to be some internal mechanism (if you listen to that piece of God inside) that speaks to you about fairness, justice, and rightness toward others. You may blunt, ignore, or bury the feeling, but it is still there, still a part of your design. Even if you have allowed anger, resentment, envy, fear, or disappointment to ravage your heart and soul, this piece of your design doesn't disappear.

We often want to say or do something when people are not being treated fairly, when there is a need for someone to stand up and help. Do you believe this desire is part of you—part of your design? It may not always be prudent or safe to say something or to take action, but when you do—when you allow that part of your design to express itself—you come closer to realizing the purpose of your life and fulfilling your intended destiny.

Some people seem to be born with bravery in their genes—taking actions to fight for, help, or protect others. Not me; I'm not inclined to put myself in harm's way in defense of others. And life circumstances have not often put me in circumstances where I would need to show the kind of bravery where one does for others at physical risk to oneself.

In my imaginings as a kid, I would make-believe I was like Audie Murphy, saving fellow soldiers in battle. I imagined myself pulling people from a burning car, and I imagined swimming through waves to save a drowning child. Those opportunities never materialized, and if they did, I always wondered how I would have really responded.

I recall the day in 1969 when draft numbers were selected in a lottery, based on birthdays, and being incredibly relieved to see that I had a high number and didn't need to worry about being sent to fight in the Vietnam War. I felt for others who were not so lucky as they sat in silence, staring out into space, or as they spoke about their fears and whether they should flee to Canada if called upon to serve.

Yes, as a teenager, I stood up to bullies who saw me as easy prey, given my height and proneness to be mouthy, or when situations were forced on me and I had no way to retreat. I have a very fond memory of Glen Shulkin, an older and much larger neighborhood kid, who picked me up and proudly carried me around on his shoulders after I successfully, and finally, confronted an older bully who continually teased me and pushed me around.

My nature was to avoid potentially violent situations and people whenever I could, letting my distaste of being hurt and bloodied prevail over my pride.

I recall in high school being part of a group that was going to fight those from another town. I let myself slowly trail behind, and at what felt like the right moment, I turned and walked home.

But I admired those who stood up for causes they believed in, despite physical threats, despite death threats—Martin Luther King for one, who had been killed in 1968, and Andrew Goodman, Michael Schwerner, and James Chaney, who in 1964, were killed by the KKK, standing up for what they believed.

My father taught me that all people were equal, and through him, I became aware and sensitive to racial discrimination.

He made it even more personal by telling me about being denied opportunities because he was Jewish. One story involved my parents traveling south, walking into a fancy hotel, and being told that Jews were not allowed—Jews were not welcome.

But I knew that no matter how much I would imagine, I was not the one to take the kind of physical risks that King, Goodman, Schwerner, and Chaney took. I was not the kind of person who would stand up and say, "This is not right." But one day, I had to confront my fear of doing so.

I was walking alone late at night and witnessed a black student who was surrounded and being taunted and threatened by a group of young white men: "Nigger! Porch monkey!"

I froze, stared, seethed with anger—everything about what I was witnessing and hearing violated my sense of rightness. But my mind was caught between two conflicting beliefs—stand up or play it safe, confront or not to confront, speak up or turn my back and ignore the injustice.

From a safe distance, I spoke up, loudly saying, "Stop! This is not right."

Everything stopped—everyone stopped. Eyes turned toward me. The black student began to walk away, slowly, then more quickly. Seconds felt like minutes and hours. "Fuck it," one in the group said. That was my cue. I quickly walked in another direction, away from the group—listening, trying to determine if I needed to run, believing (knowing) that I could outrun them, if needed.

My father would have been proud of me that day. He would have been.

But I would not have had the courage of Sergio Consuegra, who was driving home from church in 2013 and came upon a gang of angry motorcyclists who had dragged a man from his SUV on a New York City street and were pummeling him with helmets, fists, and kicks (blood flowing as he lay motionless on the ground) and were now trying to pull his wife from the car as the couple's baby screamed from the backseat. From the crowd that was watching, Consuegra stepped close to the scene, hands up, and said, "That's it, guys. Let it go! Let it go!" And they did. Later he said, "I felt that God was with me there."

Standing up for people in need doesn't have to be this dramatic—it rarely is. Equally painful can be rumors and untruths told like a sword piercing the heart, or cruel words that cut to the core, or exclusion causing loneliness and doubt, or no one seeming to care when the weight of life feels unbearable. Have you experienced this?

For Reflection and Discussion

1. Do you believe that standing up when people are in need, through words or actions, strengthens your soul and moves you closer to fulfilling your intended destiny?

2. Has someone stood up for you in your time of need? How did you feel about that person and what he or she did for you?

3. Has someone failed to stand up for you in your time of need when they should have or could have? If yes, how did you feel?

4. Have you ever stood up for others in their time of need? If yes, how did you feel about yourself?

5. Have you ever failed to stand up for others in their time of need when you should have? If yes, how did you feel about yourself?

CHAPTER 33

Don't Compromise Important Values

Many people have written and spoken about the importance of living out your values. Mahatma Gandhi was one of those individuals: "Your beliefs become your thoughts. Your thoughts become your words. Your words become your actions. Your actions become your habits. Your habits become your values. Your values become your destiny."

Do you believe that when you don't live with goodness in your heart, when you don't do right by people, you damage your soul and its development, making it more difficult to achieve the purpose of your life and your intended destiny? Do you believe you can reverse the damage done to your soul by doing what is good and right? Do you believe that God presents you with moments that become opportunities to strengthen or degrade your soul?

Important life lessons clearly come from big moments, but I have learned that simple encounters are sometimes packed with equally important messages.

Diane and I went to graduate school together at the State University of New York at Albany. We thought we had saved enough money to get us through the first year at school. By March, we were running out of funds. We got jobs. Diane worked in a credit office and as a substitute teacher. My job involved working four hours five nights a week in a factory that turned old clothing into cotton to be sold and reused.

I was responsible for operating a machine that seemed to be the size of a small house. It had metal cylinders with protruding metal spikes that worked in opposite directions to each other. The old clothing passed through the spikes, which tore and separated the fibers, producing a continuous stream of cotton that landed in a barrel.

Several times each night, I had to press the button on the wall that turned off the power to my machine to do maintenance. This involved lying on my back, shimmying under the cylinders, and using a sharp switchblade knife to cut away cotton fibers that had built up. If I didn't do this maintenance, the protruding spikes would not work properly. When I was under the machine cutting away cotton fibers, my face was only a few inches from the cylinders and protruding spikes.

One week into the job, I met a young man in his mid-twenties who had been working at the factory since turning eighteen. His father also worked at the factory, as did other relatives. I don't recall what his job was, but I do recall him telling me that he was set for life.

"How so?" I asked.

He held up his right hand; several fingers were missing. I tried hard not to overreact to the stubble he proudly displayed.

"How did it happen?"

"I was working one of the machines, slid under to clean the cotton fibers from the cylinders, and the machine turned on."

Fifteen days into the job, I turned off the power to my machine, shimmied under it, and was picking away at tangled fibers when my machine started up. Fortunately my hands were down. I quickly slid out, emerging to see a supervisor walking into the next room. I chased after him.

"Why did you turn the machine on?" I yelled so he could hear me above the roaring of the machines.

"Because it was off!" he yelled in return.

"It was off because I turned it off to clean the cylinders!" I yelled back.

"Sorry. Go back to work."

He turned and walked away. Ten minutes later, I shut off the power to my machine, left my post, found the supervisor, gave him the knife, and quit.

That night as I lay in bed, I couldn't stop thinking about that young man who felt that he was set for life—about how much he limited and compromised himself, about the price he paid for it, and about the supervisor and how he didn't seem to care. Was he that noncaring? How, I thought, do people become that way?

I needed to find another job—fast. Standing out from the other ads in the newspaper, boxed in dark gray lines, I read: "Sales—$600 per month guaranteed." The job was selling Kirby vacuum cleaners. I did well in the interview, passed the test, and fit the profile.

Each day I would go on sales calls to demonstrate the Kirby. Appointments were scheduled. People often agreed to sales presentations because they were offered a free gift. All I had to do was show up and demonstrate the Kirby.

Back then, the Kirby was very expensive—more than $500, I recall, maybe $1,000. But it was more than a vacuum cleaner. It was an entire system that included an upright and a canister vacuum, a carpet shampooer, a floor polisher, and even a paint sprayer, I think.

The Kirby came in multiple boxes because it could do so many different things and had all sorts of attachments. It took several days of training and practice to learn how to assemble and disassemble the various components, work them properly, and get them back into the boxes.

Like the guy making the pitch on TV who makes it look so easy, once mastered, I was ready to hit the road. Demonstrations (sales calls) were mostly in the evening and included vacuuming the floor after people used their old vacuums; pointing out the dirt the Kirby picked up that theirs didn't; showing the value of having a machine that could do many jobs, emphasizing the cost savings over time; explaining how the Kirby didn't need vacuum bags, which was an additional savings; and vacuuming a mattress, pointing out, as a disclaimer, that I was not medically trained to make such observations, but they were sleeping on dead skin cells their vacuum cleaners didn't suck up, but the Kirby did.

For my 7:00 p.m. appointment, I drove into a section of Albany, New York, that I should not have been in. I was nervous. This was the inner-city ghetto. I found the house, knocked on the door, and was greeted by a middle-aged black woman who let me in. Beyond her, the two things I quickly noticed were an ironing board in the dining room and clothes piled high on the dining room table.

I carried the various boxes with all the Kirby attachments into the living room, where several children were doing homework. The woman was obviously poor—no way could she afford this expensive machine. "In and out quickly," I said to myself.

I completed my demonstration, including vacuuming one of her mattresses. She was very impressed. She wanted to buy the Kirby. She asked the price. I told her what the cost would be. She shook her head. I could see her disappointment. She couldn't afford it. I felt bad.

She offered me something to drink. I accepted a cup of tea. We talked. She told me that her husband worked two jobs and that she cleaned houses during the day and did laundry and ironing for others in the evening. She told me about each of her kids and how she wanted them to go to college, to have better lives.

I told her about my upbringing, being newly married, and the factory job I had just quit; how Diane and I were running out of money and needed to earn some; about being in graduate school to earn my degrees in education and counseling; and my desire to help people.

I felt bad for her and told her so. I apologized for demonstrating this very expensive machine that she couldn't afford, making her feel bad, and making her feel guilty about not having a home that was clean enough.

"Don't feel bad for me; feel bad for yourself," she said, with no animosity.

"Why?" I asked. "What do I have to feel bad about?"

"I may be poor, but I don't compromise myself," she said. "But you have. You're doing work that you're not proud of doing. You feel guilty going into people's homes and showing them that their homes are not clean. You say you want to be a counselor who helps people, yet, for money, you're doing work that makes you feel guilty. Don't feel bad for me; feel bad for yourself, for compromising yourself and what you believe, for doing work that you feel is not right, just to make money."

Compromising, I was beginning to realize, can take many forms.

Twenty years later, her words returned to me when the CEO of a new corporate client asked me to compromise my values about doing right by people, when he asked me to mislead executives we were recruiting by telling them falsehoods. I told the CEO that what he was suggesting wasn't right to do to people. He told me to just go along, emphasizing that I could make a lot of money doing the work the way he wanted. I couldn't and lost that client and a lot of revenue.

It has taken me many years to learn the lesson from what the woman said to me that evening. I learned that when I compromise values that are important to me, when I bury the goodness that is part of my design, my self-esteem and soul degrade. Truth is, I haven't always been strong enough to practice this realization. But when I do, there is tremendous satisfaction; and when I don't, I have had regrets.

For Reflection and Discussion

1. Do you believe you can damage your soul and its development by compromising on doing what is good and right?

2. Do you believe that such compromising can end up being a source of development of your soul? If yes, how have you developed yourself and your soul through experiences when you compromised doing what is good and right?

CHAPTER 34

Don't Drift Too Far From Home

It's easy to get caught up in the moment, in the pursuit of success and hoped-for rewards or the realities of the situation we are in. We are all subject to this, some more than others. We all, from time to time, drift too far from home, losing our way, jeopardizing the development of our souls and moving us away from how we have been designed.

Have you ever drifted too far or lost your way? Most of us have. It is part of being human.

You can learn from the times when you don't do right, don't express goodness, and don't live according to your values. You can make course corrections that return you to how you have been designed. And when you do, you will come closer to achieving the purpose of your life and your intended destiny. No matter how long it takes.

The following story illustrates this by describing an important moment in my life that led to a major change.

Basketball and March can't get any better, starting with conference tournaments, continuing through the full days of early-round NCAA Championship games to the Final Four. I would arrange my work schedule to be able to watch as much basketball as possible. These one-and-done games multiply the intensity, passion, energy, and drama—it's all there, making for great theater.

To watch as many of these games as possible, I would often tell candidates I had to interview that I was not available, that I had something else scheduled, not being specific as to what. Sometimes I would tell the clients the same. I would get done what I could in the morning and stockpile the rest.

I was not able to see all the games. Sometimes work priorities or other responsibilities trumped game watching, but for the most part, each March produced significant hiatuses—gaps in my work schedule.

I'm not just talking about the men's games. In December 1993, I became rabidly hooked on UConn women's basketball after watching them beat the then-perennial powerhouse, Virginia.

Watching the quality of play from the UConn women's basketball team is pure joy. Once old-time Boston Celtic fans began watching how these UConn Women Huskies whip the ball around, working like a well-oiled machine, they would say, "These women play like the old Bob Cousy, John Havlicek, Bill Russell, and Sam and KC Jones Celtics." And the young women make you proud, not only as players, but as likable people. You watch them arrive as freshmen and develop over four years, get married, and have kids—like daughters, many of us fans say and feel.

This is why I was a bit frustrated when I had to travel to New York City for a meeting with a client who insisted we meet face-to-face to discuss a candidate I evaluated and recommended and whom he had interviewed for a vice president of operations position. It was opening March Madness day, when many games begin at noon and go through midnight.

The client was a tough, powerful, insensitive CEO and president who had a reputation for being petulant, which made him very difficult. He wanted what he wanted when he wanted it, and he was used to getting it.

We met at 11:00 a.m. in the restaurant of the hotel where he was living. We sat at a private table in the back corner, Mafia Don-like, with staff attending to his every need.

He got right to the point: "I like the candidate, but I don't hire midgets."

"Midget?" I asked, a bit perplexed, wondering what constituted a midget in his mind.

"A Napoleon complex," he went on to say. "I won't hire a midget. They have a Napoleon complex."

I am 5'7", and the candidate was probably 5'6." "What is the midget cutoff in this guy's mind?" I wondered as I sat up straighter to make myself seem taller.

I said, "Short people who might have a Napoleon complex are out to prove themselves. You might get more for your money, not less."

"More for the height," he said sarcastically. "Don't like midgets."

We went round and round about this for a while, with me trying to get him to see the whole person instead of just the person's height. I pointed out what the candidate had accomplished, his natural talents, skills, knowledge, and relevant work experience and successes.

He didn't budge, didn't give an inch.

"Napoleon complex, midget," he kept repeating, like a mantra.

Then I asked, "Am I a midget? He's not much taller than me."

"You're close," he said. "You just make the cutoff."

"What a jerk this president is—this client," I said to myself, "but he is my client and is paying me—our company—a lot of money." I dutifully responded.

From there I went to a late lunch with an executive vice president from whom I was trying to secure business. I set up the meeting through a referral. We met in his office for a few minutes and then went to a private executive dining room overlooking Central Park. What a great view. We talked about him, his life, his kids, his career, and what was important to him. Then we discussed sports—golf and tennis. Good connecting, good bonding. His company sponsored events.

It was NCAA March Madness time in 2004, and miraculously both the UConn men's and women's basketball teams went on to win national championships—the only Division 1 school in America to have done so.

"I can get you tickets to the men's or women's games," I told the EVP. "Our company makes a sizable donation to UConn and buys season tickets to both the men's and women's games." It was a bit of marketing bribery on my part.

"Maybe men, but not the women," he said.

Enthusiastically, I babbled about the UConn women's team, their skills, and how they were like daughters. When I get on a roll about the women's team and the players, I know I can overdo it, but my enthusiasm is so real, so genuine, so supportive, and so very obvious.

He cut me off midstream, dismissing me like an annoying fly.

"I would never let my daughter play basketball," he said.

"Why not?"

"They're all lesbians. All women athletes are lesbians."

My jaw dropped from his incredible rudeness, my stomach tightened, heat rose to my face, and my fists clenched under the table. I thought, "I just met him, and this is what he says. He thinks he is so above everyone else that he can say what he wants to whomever he wants." I wanted to throw my Diet Coke at him. I wanted to get up and leave. I wanted to tell him off.

But didn't. I went into listening mode, looking for opportunities to make a sale, holding my disgust and anger in check, smiling and nodding.

On my way back to Connecticut, I thought about what jerks both those people were, those two highly educated and powerful executives.

Slowly I began to realize what this was saying about me. Both were offensive people whom I don't like, yet there I was, dutifully serving the first and continuing to sell the second. What did this say about me?

That night, I dreamed about being alone on a raft, adrift in the ocean, wearing tattered clothes, sunburned, parched, surrounded by salt water, with nothing to drink. I woke up thinking, "I have drifted too far from home. I'm lost at sea and need to return home. If I don't, my soul will be forever damaged, or worse—lost."

The next day I told my business partner, Kim, "I can't do this much longer. I only want to work with people—clients—I like and respect. I can't continue to compromise the way I have been."

He understood. At a much younger age, he had been forced to come to terms with his belief in God, soul, and purpose in this world

His understanding and acceptance made what I had to do easier for me but not easier for him or the future of the business we built together.

For Reflection and Discussion

1. Has the pursuit of success caused you to compromise yourself, your soul, and the inherent goodness of your design? If yes, has doing so added or diminished your feeling that your life has meaning and purpose?

SECTION 4

You Have Been Designed to Learn from Difficulties and Challenges

In section1, I emphasized that you have been designed with giftedness and the importance of understanding your giftedness and managing it well to experience meaning, purpose, and success in your life. In section 2, I emphasized that you have been designed to seek God and the value derived when you allow God to be in your life. In section 3, I emphasized that you have been designed with an inherent goodness that needs to be expressed and that when you do, you will experience greater feelings of meaning and purpose. In this next section, I emphasize that you been designed to develop yourself and your soul through difficulties and challenges. This, too, is important to understand.

All four, I believe, are key aspects to how you have been designed by God and important vehicles through which living with meaning and purpose are achieved, feelings of success are derived, and through which you will come closer to achieving your intended destiny.

CHAPTER 35

Don't Let Fear Hold You Back

Helen Keller wrote, "Character cannot be developed in ease and quiet. Only through experience of trial and suffering can the soul be strengthened." Do you believe this? Do you believe that God allows difficulties and challenges to continually come into your life to enable your soul to develop?

There will always be joy and sadness, pain and pleasure, success and failure, difficulties, disappointments, and challenges as God helps you become who you were designed to be.

Fear is one of those challenges we all face and need to overcome.

Fear can be debilitating. It can hold you back. It can prevent you from doing things you were designed to do. Do you have fears? Do they hold you back? Have you confronted those fears? Has the challenge of overcoming your fears helped you develop your soul? Have you allowed the overcoming of fear to enable you to become more of who you were designed to be? When you do, you will come closer to achieving the purpose of your life and your intended destiny.

For all my outward bravado, restlessness, and occasionally putting myself into risky situations, I am not overly confident in many areas. I often need to overcome my fears, and sometimes I succumb to them. The problem is that my mind naturally imagines the worst. These are rabbit holes I don't want to head down—thoughts and worries I seem to have little control over, causing my body to tense and my mind to doubt and at times panic.

I can vividly recall being a child, standing on the shores of Lake George as my mother paddled out in a canoe. The image of her tipping over and drowning invaded my mind. It wouldn't let go. I wouldn't move—couldn't move. I watched and waited until she safely returned. And I continually imagined my father slicing off a finger when I worked with him in his butcher shop. I would get distracted by the comings and goings and activity all around, but the image, fed by my imagination, always returned.

As a student, I had become acutely aware of the power fear can have as I felt incredibly incompetent. So I hid in the back of each classroom, afraid to commit, until that day when Steve Mocko dislodged me, poked a hole in the safe room I had constructed, and started a process of development and change in me.

As a student, I learned to avoid taking subject areas that heightened my fears, the ones that did the most insidious damage to my confidence, such as foreign language, math, and science.

Fear even raised its ugly head in sports, one of my only refuges. By my second year as a Little League baseball player, I was playing at the highest level, starting at center field and being the team's lead-off batter. First game, first pitch, a much older and bigger left-handed pitcher (Alan Schonfeld, if I recall correctly) threw a fastball that landed squarely on my elbow, hard enough that a lump immediately began to form. I trotted to first base, bruised in more places than my left elbow.

After that, each time I went to bat, in every game that had a hard-throwing fastball pitcher, the fear of being hit by a pitch was in my mind, causing me to hesitate. As I stood in the batter's box, I would imagine the ball coming my way, hitting me, causing pain. I couldn't get my mind to stop—couldn't shake it off or replace it with positive imagery.

In the eighth grade, before basketball season was to begin, I was in the gymnasium, dribbling a basketball behind my back and through my legs, as several others tried to steal the ball from me. The coach of the junior varsity basketball team was walking through the gym and stopped to watch. He invited me to try out for the junior varsity team. I did, and I made the team. I was the youngest and the smallest player. Mostly I sat on the bench.

At a mid-season game, the junior varsity team played before the men's game. By the second half, the crowd had grown close to full capacity. Our starting point guard was not playing well, nor was the backup point guard. I was inserted into the game. I had the ball in my hand, crossed over the midcourt line, and a split second later, the ball was stolen from me, and I was chasing the other player as he dribbled toward his basket for an easy score. As he went up for the layup, I came from behind and blocked the ball out of bounds. The crowd cheered.

Then I looked down to see that one of my sneaker laces was untied. As I knelt to tie it, the referee stood over me, whistle in his mouth, holding the basketball, and the crowd watched and waited. My fingers fumbled and then shook—over and over, again and again and again, as I tried to tie those laces. It felt like an eternity. My self-consciousness leapt to a stratospheric level. Heat rose to my face, which had turned bright red. Fear of being in front of a crowd was now buried deeply inside. It was as if the chemistry in my brain changed. Hesitancy and fear, brought on by imagining the worst—intense self-consciousness—always crept in.

I learned that sometimes you can't escape, no matter how much you try. When my brother, Gene, got married, he asked me to be his best man. At the reception, one of Gene's friends asked when I was going to make the best man's toast. I didn't know I had to. I had nothing prepared. I was panicked. I ran to safety, hiding in the men's room, behind a bathroom stall, trying to decide what to do, what to say. Two of Gene's closet friends found me, coaxed me out of hiding, and suggested things for me to say. There was no escape. I stood before the group and began to speak. People laughed at what I said—as I told the truth about not knowing I had to make a best man's toast and how I hid in the bathroom stall, trying to think of things to say. As people laughed, my mind came alive with thoughts.

As satisfying as the outcome was, I felt that I had escaped a bullet (as the saying goes) and vowed never again to stand before others to give a speech. The risk was not worth the reward, or so I felt.

During my first year of employment at Saint Joseph College, a group of home economists invited me to make a speech on careers and job hunting. It was my first speech as a professional, and I was scared—terrified—but also excited by the prospect. My mixed feelings battled each other.

I wrote the entire speech on index cards so I would not make a mistake or leave something out—the fear of doing so was overwhelming. I grew to regret agreeing to do the speech, but I was determined to overcome my fear.

As I prepared—writing and rewriting, to get it perfect—my mind imagined the worst: people sitting glumly, bored, disinterested.

As I stood before the group of roughly fifty people and began to speak, my fears became reality. What I had imagined is what I saw: no interest or reaction—just blank eyes and stares. There was no escape. I continued speaking, but panic was taking over.

Without thinking, and trusting my instincts and in-the-moment reaction, I walked toward the middle of the room, took all my index cards, and tossed them in the air, loudly saying, "This is boring, isn't it? Would you rather just ask me questions?"

Slowly a hand raised and a question was asked. I responded and asked questions in return, which triggered more questions. The pace quickened. Ideas and observations came to my mind, which I used to keep the evening exciting for me and for them. My confidence in standing before others—reacting, responding, and facilitating—soared. It fit my giftedness, my MAP, but I wasn't aware of SIMA back then.

In contrast, giving a speech with no audience interaction and reaction caused all sorts of fearful thoughts and confidence issues. So I avoided giving speeches, unless I could quickly turn the session into a free-for-all discussion. Periodically I would try just giving a speech, and most times I would regret having done so.

This began to change in 2004, when my daughter, Katie, and son-in-law, Mike, asked me to speak at their wedding. I had more than two years of advanced notice, but I wrote the speech the night they asked. For the next two years, I practiced almost every day. I so wanted it to go well. It had become a main priority of mine. But no one knew how fearful I was about standing before a large group and making a speech. I worked hard at replacing negative thoughts with positive imagery—visualizing the audience (our guests) interested and responding positively and emotionally to what I was saying.

I had the speech totally memorized but still kept the pages in front of me the day I delivered it. Without the words in front of me, I knew I would freeze and forget what to say. I fought that image and tried replacing it with another image each time it appeared in my mind. I fought other involuntary images: pages out of order, pages being blown away by the wind (it was an outdoor ceremony), and losing my place, resulting in my stuttering and stumbling. In each scenario, I saw the faces of those attending, staring blankly in amazement at my incompetence.

The speech was heartfelt, emotional, and well-received. It touched people's emotions and garnered positive reactions afterward.

All I focused on as I spoke were the emotion and pride I saw and felt in the eyes of Katie and Mike. It was their moment, and I didn't want my fear to ruin it. They didn't know I was in a total panic, which melted away as I began saying the first few words.

There were other times, though, when fear prevailed. In the early 1990s, I received a telephone call from a producer at *The TODAY Show*. Katie Couric was going to do a story on bosses. The producer explained that they had seen several quotes I made that appeared in the *Hartford Courant*—thus the telephone call. Katie Couric would be doing the interview. I could drive down to New York City or go to the local NBC affiliate in the Hartford area. I was in love with Katie Couric's personality and style. I so wanted to meet her and do the interview, but I kept imagining the camera on me causing me to freeze or say something dumb.

Remembrances of moments when I felt paralyzed rushed to my mind, self-conscious moments like that basketball game when I couldn't get my sneaker laces tied and another that happened when I was a college freshman, enamored with a cute blonde girl who was trying out for a part in a play. I went along, agreed to read a few lines, and was given a small role—Nutsy in the play *The Male Animal*.

I had maybe twenty words to say. I was panicked, and no matter how much I tried, I found it difficult to remember my lines. Panic blocked what little memorizing ability I had. My solution: write my lines on a chalkboard that I placed behind the curtain, by the location where I entered the stage, so I could read them just before I was to say them. But even that didn't help. I flubbed my lines and stood embarrassed but was quickly saved by the seasoned performers who flawlessly adapted. I knew I never wanted to be in that kind of visibly embarrassing position again.

I declined the offer to appear on *The TODAY Show*, babbling some excuse, eventually admitting that I would not be good on TV—that I would panic.

Fear of the unknown, of making a mistake, looking foolish, or failing can be overwhelming. I always regretted that decision.

Several years later, in 2001, after I wrote the first edition of my book *Managing Yourself, Managing Others*, I was invited to appear on a local television show. I declined, but the host of the show asked, "Why won't you accept the invitation?" I explained my fear to him. He told me that the studio was set up like a living room, with us sitting in two chairs, angled to face each other. "You will hardly notice the camera," he said, persuasively encouraging and convincing me to move past my hesitancy and fear—to step out of my comfort zone.

My mind ran rampant, the whole time, prior to when I was scheduled to appear on his television show. I fought the compelling urge to back out.

The recording studio was set up like a living room, but I did notice the cameras. A lump formed in my throat, but it went well. I was proud of overcoming my fear.

Radio interviews were different. No one could see me, and all I had to do was spontaneously respond to questions.

In 1997, I met Kenny Klepper while doing a retained executive search for United Healthcare. My assignment was to help hire a new senior vice president of operations. The president of United Healthcare's Uniprise Division, the person to whom the position would report, gave me Kenny's name. After interviewing Kenny, I felt that he would not be highly motivated by the job when I compared his MAP to the position profile described to me. Kenny agreed with my assessment of him and the kind of work situations he would thrive in.

Kenny is a large-scale and bold change agent who often pushes beyond limits and boundaries. He did it with operational functions, products, businesses, himself, people, and eventually, me. We hit it off wonderfully, and he eventually hired me as a consultant, initially at Empire Blue Cross, where he was working when we first met, and then at Medco Health Solutions, where he had become president.

Over a seven-year-period at Medco, my company worked with more than five hundred Medco employees, and the work didn't end until 2012, when Medco was acquired by ExpressScripts.

A few years into my consulting with Medco, Kenny called and said, "I want you to speak at Medco's annual management meeting."

"How many people?" I asked.

"Four hundred, maybe five hundred," he said.

I immediately went into an intense panic, not only because it was a speech but also because the number of people expected to be in the audience felt completely overwhelming to me.

I explained to Kenny that I couldn't make the speech, despite the opportunity and potential. I had to diminish myself in his eyes. I had to decline his offer. I had to get out of it.

Without hesitating, Kenny said, "Don't worry. I'll be on the stage with you. I'll have others there also, and you don't need to prepare anything."

He was so persuasive that I couldn't say no.

On that day, I stood on the stage with Kenny and four Medco executives, all of whom I had done consulting for. I didn't know what to expect.

Kenny introduced me by telling the story about my interviewing and recommending against his taking the senior executive role at United Healthcare. He joked about how I cost him a lot of money in compensation, how he hired me as a consultant, and how the work I did expanded. He said he wanted those in the audience to be aware of my philosophy and process, to know how valuable it has been to the company and him personally, and how the four executives on stage would tell about their experiences with me and the process.

I enjoyed listening to the accolades—getting caught up in hearing about myself. Suddenly Kenny turned and said, "Steve, explain the work you do. Describe the process and its scope and usage at Medco."

As he said that, his eyes twinkled, and he smiled. He trusted me. He knew I could handle it. He wouldn't let my own fear and doubts hold me back. I had no time to imagine the worst. New ground had been broken.

On another day, Kenny called and said, "I want to make a video about the work you did for us, to be included in a gift package to be given to those who have gone through your MAP assessment and coaching process."

"That's a good idea," I said.

"I want you to do the video with me."

I thought about how I avoided appearing on *The TODAY Show* and how I flubbed my lines in the college play. My instincts were to decline, but I didn't, and I didn't tell Kenny that I feared going before the camera.

Whenever my mind begins to run rampant with images of saying dumb and stupid things, I visualize myself on stage in front of four hundred to five hundred Medco executives, spontaneously saying the right words. I visualize myself speaking before two hundred guests at my daughter's wedding and evoking an emotional response. And I visualize myself speaking on camera and on radio broadcasts and people listening with interest.

Fear, I have come to understand, has a way of protecting us, sometimes justifiably and sometimes unnecessarily. It also has a way of diminishing performance or holding one back, but it can also produce enhanced concentration or needed growth and change.

I've learned to work hard at pushing away the negative imagery as best I can, replacing it with positive imagery, and trusting myself, just as Kenny trusted me. And I've learned to accept that my fearful imaginings are reflective of my giftedness—my MAP—part of my design. I learned that my anticipatory "What if?" thinking doesn't have to rule me; it doesn't have to hold me back from doing things I was designed to do.

For Reflection and Discussion

1. If you let it, fear can prevent you from doing things you are gifted to do and designed to do. It can stunt the development of your soul and hold you back from achieving your purpose and fulfilling your intended destiny. Has this been the case for you?
2. How did you feel when you allowed fear to hold you back?
3. How did you feel when you didn't allow fear to hold you back?
4. What fears are holding you back now? What will you do about it?

CHAPTER 36

Avoid Being Resentful

Is there something about yourself that you don't like? How about something you hate about yourself and have grown to resent? If yes, you are not alone. None of us, I have come to understand through my interviewing, is without blemish; everyone has one or more things about themselves they wish were different. Some hide their feelings, while others have allowed their anger, disappointment, and resentment to grow out of proportion, as I did. This, if not reined in and put in perspective, can eat away at your soul and prevent you from achieving your purpose and fulfilling your intended destiny.

Sleep sometimes comes upon me—within seconds—without much warning. I might be listening, observing, or reading, and suddenly my mind shuts down, my eyes close, and my head falls. Most times I can halt the process by jolting myself to a degree of attentiveness—the battle continuing —but sometimes I wake up a few seconds later, very aware that I have fallen asleep. Other times I fall fast asleep for several minutes, waking up dismayed that it happened again. This has plagued me my entire life, for as long as I can remember, starting in school.

As I moved into a full-time work schedule, I quickly recognized that high doses of caffeine helped counter the problem. That is when I began medicating myself—as if I were using a hospital drip. I drank tea all morning, Diet Coke all afternoon, and occasionally spiked it all with coffee. Later, I graduated to caffeine pills.

As I write this, I recall taking a diet pill in college to be able to study; its effect on my ability to concentrate was remarkable. I know that people with ADHD take similar kinds of stimulant medication, but I also understand that I have an addictive personality, and I would easily have grown too dependent on those strong stimulants. For that reason, I am grateful that they were not readily and legally available to me at the time. Caffeine became my drug of choice.

I also found that short naps of twenty minutes or less fend off this intense, sudden need to sleep. After the nap, I am able to focus and concentrate with great intensity.

As the caffeine spikes lasted less time, I learned how best to manage my caffeine intake and naps. I tinkered with the timing and amount of each, depending on my tiredness and my schedule.

Even now, if I am not fresh from a nighttime of sleep or a nap, or loaded up on caffeine, reading is difficult, causing an inability to focus. Drowsiness, and eventually sleep, takes over.

I try, as best I can, to do all my reading and mental-concentration work early each day and save the afternoon for discussions, sales calls, telephone conversations, and physical activity that I assess has the kind of pace and intensity to serve as a natural stimulant.

Over time, and after much denial, I began to think that I had some form of mild narcolepsy, but I didn't want anyone to know, even though some jokingly mentioned it.

For the most part, I am successful in managing it all, but at times, sleep just happens, despite my best efforts.

Sometimes, briefly during a conversation, my head suddenly drops, my body sags, and I fall asleep. With some friends and family, it is a source of jokes. As they see me struggling to stay awake, they offer me their couch. Usually I remain in the chair and nod off for a few minutes.

I learned to take preventive naps whenever possible: before meetings, interviews, social engagements, and long drives. Diane often reminds me to do so before driving long distances. Even a thirty-second nap can restart my clock and refresh me. Sometimes I put the car I am driving into the park gear when I'm stopped at a red light and ask Diane to wake me when the light turns green. I close my eyes, and within a second, I am fast asleep. Thirty seconds or one minute later, Diane wakes me—I am totally refreshed.

I learned that standing and walking around during interviews helps, and to some extent, so does asking questions and promising people my instant assessment. This is like walking on a tightrope with no netting below; it creates tension and acts as a stimulant for me.

Over time, I began to understand that a lack of pace drains my energy and increases the chances of my falling asleep. In contrast, opportunities that involve intense and engaging activity—something new, challenging, unknown, risky, or physical, like sports—is an antidote.

I spent many years resenting this aspect of myself and wishing I were different. This caused anger, frustration, and disappointment to grow within me, in who I am.

Eventually, I came to accept this *thing* about me that I hated and resented. I learned to accept myself—with all the good and bad. And with acceptance came peace of mind and spirit.

I learned that the kind of resentment I felt is not healthy, whether it is obvious or lingering below the surface; it eats away at the soul. And when that happens, we drift farther away from our intended destinies and who we are designed to be.

For Reflection and Discussion

1. Is there something you hate or resent about yourself, or that you did hate or resent? If yes, how has it affected your life and the development of your soul? How has it prevented you from becoming all that God designed you to be?

CHAPTER 37

Don't Allow Loss to Weaken Your Soul

Loss can be difficult to deal with at any age. It can take on many forms—death for sure, or losing a job, a limb, a capability, an argument, a game, a sense of self, or a friend, to name a few. Loss brings on many emotions and challenges. It can be a trap door to fall through or a spark for change and hopefully growth and development. Loss can be an anchor that holds you down or an opportunity to come closer to achieving the purpose of your life and your intended destiny.

Peter Hendelman was six and I was five when we met. He lived next door. One year later, he moved up the road to live in his grandmother's home, just a one-minute walk away. He was lanky and much taller than me. His father was a musician. Peter always wore thick glasses, a T-shirt, ragged jeans, and torn sneakers. We were inseparable, best friends.

We had our bikes and long summer days of exploring. To the north was the Great Woods, stretching east and west, eventually connecting to the Great Desert in the western corner.

Each week, Peter and I would take our small allowances and ride our bikes fifteen minutes down the Boulevard to Bargain Town, where we would buy bags of little green rubbery soldiers. By summer's end, we had hundreds, if not thousands, of those little green men, posed in all sorts of fighting positions. We would stage them for battles and then release aerial bombardments of rocks and see who survived our attacks. We continually made war noises and laughed and laughed.

Each day, we left our homes in the morning and returned at dinner time, free to roam and do whatever—what a wonderful feeling.

The fastest way to get to the Great Desert was to ride our bikes down the paved street that Peter and I lived on to the end and then take the path, through the weeds, in the swampy area that ended at a dirt road.

This dirt road was covered with potholes that always seemed to have muddy water in them. Every now and then, a pickup truck would bounce down the road. In many ways, it was a lonely road, having no important functions and leading to no important places.

It would take us twenty minutes, sometimes more, to reach the Great Desert. Along the way, we would examine abandoned refrigerators, rusty cars, and other items.

We called this parcel of land, which was probably no larger than a quarter mile wide and long, a desert because of its white sand. It stood out, bounded by a salt water channel to its north and west, eventually bending south toward the Atlantic Ocean, and the Great Woods, which spread for miles to the northeast. Seagulls walked along the shore and glided through the air, occasionally diving into the channel in search of food.

When Peter and I arrived at the desert, we would drag our bikes across and sneak to the shore, trying not to disturb the seagulls, and take the higher ground. Using rocks we had put in our pockets along the way, we would let loose a barrage on those poor birds, who became an imaginary Nazi air force and we the courageous American ground artillery. We never hit a bird.

When the beach cleared, we would sit on the shore, remove our sneakers and socks, roll up our jeans, and wiggle our toes in the water. We would throw rocks into the water, skipping those that had smooth bottoms. Into our shirt pockets we would reach, removing cigarettes we had swiped from our parents. Smoking and feeling older than our young ages, we would wave to sailors, who waved back from slow-moving barges.

Peter and I could not sit still. So it wasn't long before we would be off again—running up and down sand dunes, waving sticks, and fighting imaginary Arabs. Fighting, running, and rolling in the sand was so much a part of this Lawrence of Arabia land.

During one of these battles, Peter and I saw an arm protruding from underneath a sand dune. Hesitantly, we approached, prodding the limb with a stick. We cautiously inspected it and determined it was not made of flesh.

Using our hands as shovels, we dug deep into the sand and withdrew a body. It was a straw-filled scarecrow. We named him Oscar, and he gave us quite an experience.

We cleared Oscar away from the sand. Scattered around Oscar, buried in the sand, was discarded wood. As we left for the day, leaving Oscar lying on the sand for the buzzards and ants, we turned to say good-bye.

"He looks real," I said.

"He does, doesn't he?" Peter replied.

Down the road and halfway home, I said to Peter, "If Oscar looks real to us, wouldn't he look real to the people on the barges and who drive the pickup trucks?" By the time we reached our homes, our devious minds had created a nasty little plan.

The next morning, our miniature workingmen's hands and pockets carried nails, a hammer, a saw, and some rope—as much as we could manage to grasp and haul.

We dragged Oscar and the wood that was buried with him to the top of the highest sand dune. By late morning, we began to build the most awkward-looking and unstable scaffold any hangman could be asked to use. Oscar wouldn't mind.

At dusk, standing on the edge of the Great Desert, just off the dirt road, we turned and stared at Oscar. He was swinging by his neck in a slight breeze, contrasting perfectly with the darkening sky.

We were young and innocent and laughed at the entertaining thought of what the passing sailors or drivers of the pickup trucks would think when they saw Oscar hanging and at the image of them running through the desert to cut straw-headed Oscar down.

Following a long night of anticipation, we hurried back to the scene of the crime. In the distance we saw our scarecrow hanging, but not as we had left him.

Through the desert we crawled, and up the sand dune we slithered. Peeking over the top of the dune, we peered at Oscar. He was hanging by his feet. I looked at Peter, and Peter looked at me.

"Is that how we left him?" I asked.

"I don't think so," Peter said.

"Maybe someone turned him over?"

"Look for footprints."

"I don't see any," I said.

"I don't, either."

"How could someone turn him over without leaving footprints behind?" I asked, lost for an answer.

"They can't," Peter said.

We cut straw-headed Oscar down and dismantled the scaffold. By late morning, Peter and I sat across from our straw man, whom we had propped into a sitting position.

"Did we hang him by his feet?" I asked.

"No."

"Did we see any footprints?"

"No."

"How can that be unless..."

"Are you alive?" Peter asked the scarecrow.

"Do you think he'd tell us?" I asked.

"Why not?"

"After we hung him?"

"I forgot about that."

"What should we do with him?"

Peter jumped to his feet and said, "Let's go home. I've got an idea."

As we walked home, Peter explained his idea. "Poor Oscar," I thought. Hanging just wasn't enough.

"But what if he's real?" I asked.

Peter's reply—"He isn't; don't worry"—enabled both of us to concentrate on refining and perfecting the idea.

We returned the next day with two bottles of ketchup and an enormous meat knife. We placed them at the foot of a boulder that lay in the middle of a wide circular bend just off the dirt road. We carried Oscar to the boulder and placed him on top of it. On his back. We took the enormous meat knife and thrust it into Oscar's stomach. We took the ketchup and poured it about the strawman's belly and over the side of the boulder facing the dirt road.

I awoke that night sweating in a nightmarish fever of invading Oscars. Morning and Peter calmed me down.

We could not believe our eyes as our mouths gaped open. There sat Oscar, his back against the boulder, ketchup and knife gone. Our eyes bulged without blinking. We did not move or look at each other.

"Peter," I said.

"Yes?"

"What should we do now?"

"I don't know."

"Peter."

"Yes?"

"Do you think he's real?"

"I don't know."

We looked at each other and took off, riding our bikes away as fast as we could.

We never solved the mystery of Oscar, but the intrigue and adventure further reinforced the love and bond we had for each other.

Over time, the Great Woods and Great Desert became housing developments, shopping centers, strip malls, a golf course, a park, and a temple.

It wasn't long after our experience with Oscar that our summer came to an end and Peter moved. I never had a chance to say good-bye. I didn't know he was moving until he was gone. I recall the sadness I felt.

I think that's how it is with people who come into our lives. Some remain for a moment, some for a day, a week, a month, a year, several years, or a lifetime. People eventually move on. Their spirits become part of you, in memory and emotion, and they're sometimes gone prematurely for a reason that is hard to understand and accept. And sometimes there is an overwhelming sadness from a sense of loss that needs to be embraced and absorbed. It should not hold you back but should strengthen you, strengthen your soul, and help you move forward.

Loss, I have come to believe, forces us to reach deep inside, and it is through that process that we have the opportunity to become more of who we are designed to be.

"In the process of letting go, you will lose many things from the past, but you will find yourself," Deepak Chopra says.

For Reflection and Discussion

1. How well have you embraced and dealt with the loss of people who have been important to you? How has losing them strengthened or weakened your soul, held you back, or moved you forward?

2. Have you experienced other kinds of losses? How well have you dealt with them? Have these losses strengthened or weakened your soul, held you back, or moved you forward?

3. If these losses have held you back, what will you do to change their negative impact on you and your soul?

CHAPTER 38

Learning from Feeling Helpless

Helplessness can force many reactions; one is to reach deep inside and learn to believe and trust. The outcome may not be what you want. When it isn't, you learn to accept, and when it is, you rejoice. Either way, your soul is affected, and its development moves either forward or backward. It moves you closer or further from achieving the purpose of your life and your intended destiny.

In 1982, I would start each day the same way. Early in the morning, when all was dark, our two-year-old daughter, Katie, would gently call out, "Daddy," announcing that she was awake. I would walk across the hallway to her bedroom, open the door, sit on the top of the steps that led downstairs, and wait. A few moments later, Katie would toddle out of her darkened bedroom into my waiting arms. I would lift her off the floor and carry her down the steps.

As we descended, I would say, "Close your eyes," elongating the word *close* for effect. Her tiny fingers would tightly press against her closed eyes so no light could penetrate.

I carried her through the living room and into the kitchen, to the dimmer switch that controlled one of the kitchen lights. As I slowly moved the switch upward, Katie's fingers would spread, and her eyes would gently open, letting in the light. She would flash me a big, radiant smile, and her blue eyes twinkled as she said, "I love you, Daddy."

This was our ritual—our special moment—a wonderful way to begin each day.

Special moments don't last long—they are often fleeting and short-lived —but they remain forever. I see them in my mind, like scenes from a movie, evoking feelings that don't dissipate:

- Kevin's first Halloween, three months past his second birthday, when we dressed him up as a businessman. He wore one of Diane's old, tan corduroy sports jackets, which dragged on the ground. He had a hat on his head and a tie around his neck, and he carried a small briefcase—a sight to be seen.

- The night when Diane and I were reading to Kevin, and he to us, when three-year-old Katie said, "I can read the book." We thought she had memorized the words in the book, so we took out another book, newly purchased, and she read it. Parental pride is a wonderful feeling.

- Coming home each night from work and, without eating, going with Kevin into the carpeted and paneled side of the basement, where I had nailed to the wall, low to the ground, an old, round laundry basket that had no bottom. We played basketball. We played football, tackling each other. We crashed through walls and other structures made from cardboard bricks we had bought through the JC Penny catalog. We also played soccer and hockey and hit a giant Weeble-like blow-up football player who wouldn't stay down, always rising back up for more. We bounced a tennis ball against the walls, and we wrestled endlessly. Dinner could wait —that hour was our time.

- Riding my bike, with Kevin or Katie sitting in the child bike seat, exploring the streets, houses, parks, and school playgrounds— riding fast down hills, the wind blowing in our faces.

- The wonder on the kids' faces at Disneyworld as we floated on water through It's a Small World and flew through Journey to Imagination with Figment.

- Sliding down a water slide at Hershey Park with Kevin sitting on my lap, feeling his excitement and joy, which trumped my fear of heights, splashing into the water and seeing his triumphant smile.

- Walking along a beach in Cape Cod as the sun was setting, holding Diane's hand, watching Kevin and Katie run through the sand and splash in the water.

- Feeding baby goats at the Catskill Game Farm and lifting Katie over my head as the goats surrounded and engulfed her.

- Watching Katie jump in and out of a pile of leaves I had just raked —occasionally disappearing, worried that a car might drive by and not see her. I watched like a hawk. Her joy was infectious.

- Standing in the shallow end of a swimming pool in Florida, with Kevin and Katie diving and swimming between my legs while my father proudly watched.

- Playing catch with Kevin and Katie, just as my father did with me. I felt proud that each could handle what I tossed their way, just as my father was of me.

- Watching Katie as a six-year-old T-ball player, holding a glove that was almost as large as her. She was catching, throwing, and hitting as well as anyone, despite being a girl and the smallest person on the field. She even played the pitcher role and batted first. Parental pride can, at times, overwhelm.

- Kevin scoring a goal in soccer, pitching a win in Little League, getting a hit, catching the ball, and making a play as the point guard. My heart always pounded at those moments when his skill was being tested. Even though I was often coaching, I was always the hopeful, proud father.

- Watching Kevin boogie-boarding endlessly in the waters of Maui and then joining him—father and son riding the waves together, laughing, challenging each other, bragging, and bonding.

- Traveling the road to Hana, all four of us swimming in a pond fed by a waterfall, exploring caves, swimming in the water at the black-sand beach, and walking through rainforest vegetation as big as the kids, with Kevin narrating an imaginative adventure about searching for the magic Coke bottle. I was thinking that he would become a radio disc jockey someday.

- Getting caught in the rain and running for shelter. I can still see the kids' drenched clothing, matted-down hair, and wet, smiling faces.

- The first time Diane and I took Kevin and Katie to a Japanese restaurant and seeing the joy on their faces as the chef tossed, chopped, and maneuvered the knives with ease. Kevin struck up a conversation with the man who sat next to him, as if he were a salesman going in for the close.

- Attending plays and musicals Katie performed in and being in awe of her flawless portrayals.

- On vacation, Kevin effortlessly making friends wherever we went—particularly at the Fort Lauderdale Marriott, where as an eight-year-old, he bought an entire group of newly-made-friends' hot dogs and sodas, charging it all to my room. It wasn't so funny at the time, but the scene comes to my mind with joy as I write this. As does the time when Kevin, as a six-year old, removed all the nut-covered raisins from a box of Raisin Nut Bran and hid them in the closet in his room, in an old briefcase I had given him, in case he became hungry in the middle of the night.

- Looking through many chain-link fences as Katie played tennis matches, always against much bigger and stronger players. At times, her racquet seemed as big as her—she wasn't the best, but her spunk could not be beat.

- Watching Kevin and Katie eat lobsters at a Port Judith restaurant. They masterfully took them apart, and when they were done, I said, "I should have videotaped this." Kevin then convinced me to run to the car to get the video camera, and while I was gone, he reconstructed the lobsters.

- Frustrated, sitting against a wall, ten-year-old Katie sitting down next to me, putting her hand on my shoulder, telling me that all would get better. "Where did that empathy come from?" I asked myself. It worked—whatever was frustrating me melted away. How could it not?

These and other moments flashed through my mind, as if I were on my death bed, after eleven-year-old Katie stood in the kitchen, saying, "I can't sleep. My heart is racing."

Diane and I timed her heartbeat using the clock on the microwave; it was beating extremely fast. We called the pediatrician. He had the pediatric endocrinologist, whom Katie had seen earlier that day, call us immediately.

"Go to the all-night pharmacy and pick up two prescriptions I am going to call in," the doctor said.

"Prescriptions for what?"

"One for her thyroid and the other to get her heart rate down. And keep her awake until the medicine brings the rate down."

"Why?"

"She might die. Now, go."

Protective love is unbelievably powerful, as is that helpless feeling.

"Prayer and helplessness are inseparable. Only he who knows can truly pray," theologian Ole Hallesby wrote. As I drove to the pharmacy, I prayed.

For Reflection and Discussion

1. Do you view those moments in your life when you experience helplessness as opportunities to develop your soul, come closer to God, and come closer to achieving the purpose of your life and your intended destiny?

2. Have you ever had a helpless feeling about the health of someone you love or about yourself? How well did you handle the situation? How has it had a positive or negative impact on you, your faith, and the development of your soul?

CHAPTER 39

Don't Allow Self-Doubt to Stop You

Have you ever allowed self-doubt to hold you back from doing things you have been gifted to do? Have you allowed self-doubt to become an anchor that holds you down? Can you see overcoming self-doubt as an opportunity?

When you overcome self-doubt and pursue what you have been gifted to do, you will develop yourself and your soul and have a better chance of achieving the purpose of your life and your intended destiny.

Other than attending the occasional high school reunion, for almost forty years I didn't stay in touch with any friends from my elementary and high school years. In reflection, it may have been one of those unconscious decisions designed to protect myself.

I'm sure that many people have painful memories that have affected them as mine have done to me. All of us, I have come to realize, deal with them in our own ways. Mine were quite insidious—forever embedding in me doubts about my intelligence and capabilities—brought on by disastrous experiences and memories of school and being a student.

I have learned that the mind can be either a trap that is difficult to extricate oneself from or a wonderful tool that can draw on memories and feelings to counter doubts and insecurities.

Doubts about my intelligence and ability to measure up to others first appeared in elementary school, when I encountered difficulty understanding and following instructions, learning certain topics, and demonstrating certain capabilities like singing a song or playing a musical instrument. Even to this day, I have great difficulty remembering words to songs, and despite repeated attempts at trying to learn to play a musical instrument, I just can't.

Maybe it was in fourth grade when I was given a flute and then a trumpet—even the simplest note playing eluded me. I watched others progress. I recall one teacher who noticed my difficulty in remembering words to a song taking me aside and suggesting that I mouth it rather than try to sing out loud with others in the chorus.

Drawing and painting, fun activities for most, produced the same feelings of doubt and incompetence back then, and they still do today. Yes, I tried, even as an adult, to learn, but I gave up after the third class. I just couldn't follow what was being taught, couldn't reproduce what was in front of me or what was in my head that I so desperately wanted to draw.

All these doubts took root, firmly anchoring themselves in me at the end of the sixth grade, when I was told that I was going to be left back—left behind to do the grade over. But instead, I was allowed to go into grade seven on the condition that I perform better going forward. I knew I was different, that I was not smart, and that I was not as capable as most people, but I latched onto what I was good at—sports and later, gambling.

One day, in the midst of all this doubt, as I was walking home from high school, a friend said something to me that forever remained in my head— words I drew upon whenever I felt overwhelmed and not smart enough, even back then, when I hardly understood anything about myself. It was an innocent comment that Ed Edelson made to me as we walked home from school together.

Without prompting and for no reason, Ed looked at me and said, "You're not stupid. Why don't you work at school?"

No one had ever told me before that I was not stupid. I latched onto those words, holding them closely—using them to believe, to counter what my experiences were continually communicating to me.

So here it was, forty years after high school graduation, and I am a success, with advanced college degrees; having taught in a college and a university; being the author of a book and several articles; presentations made; and working with executives, entrepreneurs, scientists, engineers, operations, IT, sales, marketing, product development, human resources, administration—successful people from all professions—and I see Ed's name in an email. He was helping organize a high school reunion.

I was fifty-eight years old at the time and more comfortable with my past—with my journey—more accepting of my deficiencies and limitations, more confident in who I am. I sent Ed an email, reminding him of that moment, alluding to my past, telling him how much his comment and belief in me had helped me over the years, and how appreciative I was of him and his friendship back then. He wrote back, saying that he also remembered that moment and always thought that he was "pompous" for saying what he did to me. But he cared and felt he needed to say what he did. Ed and I spoke by telephone and realized that we lived only twenty minutes from each other.

After earning a bachelor's degree from Cornell University and a master's degree from Harvard University, Ed ended a very successful career as the General Manager of ExxonMobil in Bermuda. In 2004, he and his wife, Christine, opened a bed and breakfast in Southbury, Connecticut, and in 2011, he was elected First Selectman of Southbury—like a mayor.

Shortly after we reconnected, in 2007, Ed invited me to speak before his church. I accepted but was not sure if I wanted to do my standard presentation. I was in the middle of writing this book. I thought about how I had spent most of my life running from my past—creating an image and illusion about myself—how, six years earlier, I wanted to tell my story to those college and university presidents but *chickened out*. I shared all this with Ed. He encouraged me to tell my story—which became the "Unlock Your Giftedness" story in this book.

I listened to Ed's generous introductory words. He told stories to illustrate our connection and described the positive traits he saw in me in my youth as an athlete and a friend, as well as my seemingly "no care in the world" attitude. He closed by describing how one day, while walking home from school, he gave me a lecture on my lack of scholastic effort. He said that for many years afterward, he felt like a pompous fool for having done so and described how we met again, more than forty years later, and was surprised to learn that I had achieved success in my life.

I thought about how we all have different memories that stick with us— that help shape us, who we are, what we believe, and how we feel about ourselves. I thought about how lucky I was to have a friend like Ed who was caring enough to say what he did to me that day as we walked home from school together. They were words that I adopted and used to counter experiences that were telling me otherwise—that were blocking out good things about myself that I didn't yet recognize or appreciate.

Sometimes painful experiences and memories can become far more important than they are and affect us far more dramatically than they should. They often do, but they can be countered. They can become springboards, opportunities that build determination if you treat them the right way. The mind can be a wonderful tool if you allow it.

For Reflection and Discussion
1. Do you have doubts about yourself that hold you back from doing what you have been gifted to do? If yes, what are you doing about it?
2. Do you have people in your life who believe in you? Do you allow their belief in you to give you needed confidence and courage? If not, why not?
3. Are there people you know who doubt themselves? If yes, what are you doing to help them overcome their self-doubt?

CHAPTER 40

Living with and Learning from Pain

We are all given pain to deal with. No one escapes. The question is, how does it affect us? Does it move us forward or set us back? Do we grow and develop as a result, or retreat and shrink?

Frustration, anger, and resentment have a way of creeping up and becoming a way of life, ever so slowly, without even realizing that its malignant effect has taken control of emotions and mind. At least that's what happened to me. My forties were a piece of cake, but my fifties brought an onslaught I wasn't ready for.

The door opened wide when illness, and eventually death, took both my parents. I had grown to admire and appreciate their values, sacrifice, and love for each other and their love of family. They had become an important part of my life, and now they were gone. This difficult time was exacerbated by my son, who was causing significant emotional pain as he struggled with his life and growing into manhood. I was working tremendously long hours, which didn't help. It was wearing down my resistance, both physically and emotionally. To keep up the pace, I was living on caffeine, little sleep at night, and naps.

My body was also falling apart, and the implications went beyond physical pain. Playing sports, always a haven for me, now became a battle. First came heel spurs, literally making me crawl out of bed and then down the steps. It took six months for the pain to retreat. But I continued to play basketball and tennis. Then came a high ankle sprain, and I was sidelined for months.

Then came knee pain, followed by sciatica pain, which became so severe that I could barely drive the car—mostly doing so on cruise control so I could rest my right leg in such a way that the pain was minimized. Sitting was a problem. I often worked standing up. The sciatica pain lasted just short of two years. I gave up playing basketball, continued to play tennis, and began playing more golf. Then arthritis hit my back. I took so much Aleve, Advil, and Excedrin that I developed stomach pains, so the doctor prescribed Arthrotec.

To survive and overcome the back pain, I began each day with forty-five minutes of stretching and core-strengthening exercises—a routine I maintain to this day. Periodically the pain would return, and sometimes it was so severe my legs would give out and my body would crumble unless I quickly found a place to sit, or something to grab hold of, to steady myself. Then there was posterior tibular tendonitis; even simple walking was painful. It took several years of visits to physicians, physical therapists, and an orthotist and a routine of foot and ankle strengthening exercises to eventually get the pain to cease, but that, too, would return periodically. My tennis playing was greatly restricted.

Then an enlarged prostate led to urinary tract retention and a visit to the emergency room at a hospital. I learned to catheterize myself, a skill that, even in my wildest imagination, I never thought I'd have to learn. I carried a catheter and gel with me all the time, just in case. Two prostate surgeries ended that need. Between those surgeries, my retina tore, and I was sidelined for six weeks.

Following that, I developed iliotibial band syndrome, with pain running from my hip to the knee in my right leg. I added more stretching and strengthening exercises to my morning routine.

At times, I was not all that pleasant to live with. Just ask my wife, Diane. I was increasingly aware of how I was becoming—had become—and didn't like it.

I needed to write—was trying to write—about what all this was doing to me and how I reached a place of frustration and resentment, how it was beginning to skew my perceptions, how I was increasingly seeing what was negative, and how it affected the way I looked at life.

Then in 2015, as I was working on another edit of this book, shortly after turning sixty-six years of age, the back and sciatica pain returned in such an excruciating way that it made my previous bouts seem mild in comparison. Sleep became impossible. I was prescribed oxycodone, but after taking it, I had an allergic reaction in the middle of the night, causing difficulty with swallowing and breathing. I survived on my knees, hands clasped in prayer, begging God to help—to give me peace of mind, a calm heart, and the ability to accept. Calmness came. My throat relaxed. Four days later, I received my first epidural, but the pain persisted. Moderation came after a second epidural. If the pain didn't moderate, the neurosurgeon said, the next step was spinal fusion from the T10 vertebra to my pelvis.

One month later, I lost most of the stability in my right foot and ankle, which had the posterior tibular tendonitis problem. I was advised to have surgery to replace a dead tendon with one from my toes and repair another that had torn, reconstruct my heel and midfoot, repair a torn ligament, remove the arthritis from my ankle (which was described as end stage), and fuse the foot and ankle to my leg. Three screws were inserted into my ankle where it met my leg, and two metal plates were grafted into my foot—one to hold my reconstructed heel in place and the other into my midfoot to hold a newly constructed arch.

During recovery from that surgery, I discovered that I am prone to "cast claustrophobia," resulting in a confined feeling and periodic anxiety and panic attacks. This felt like hell. Eating brought on anxiety, as did the simple task of taking a drink, resulting in feeling as if I were going to choke, that my breathing would stop. I lost ten pounds in four weeks. Even the simple joy of watching TV often brought on anxious feelings. Medicine helped, but it was not enough. My mind and emotions lost control; panic overwhelmed. I prayed. That is when I admitted that I was losing the battle with my panic, that nothing I tried was working. I asked God to take over. I put myself into His hands. I asked Him to help me calm down. Relief was short-lived. God was not yet finished with me.

The "cast claustrophobia" gave way to a debilitating nerve pain in my foot. Panic and anxiety returned, joining forces with my intense nerve pain. I prayed:

> Dear God, please help me. My foot hurts; I'm in continuous pain. I'm sad, depressed, restless, anxious. I can't sleep. I lay my head down and feel the pain and anxiety. I try mindful breathing and feel the pain and, again, anxiety. I sit up. I move. I'm exhausted from a lack of sleep—so tired—twenty-four hours a day, seven days a week. I can't stop regretting that I elected to have this foot and ankle surgery. I can't walk. If I sit, there is pain. If I lie down, there

is pain. There is no relief. It's difficult to find anything to do to busy myself—to distract me. This nerve pain won't stop; it is unrelenting. I am trying to put all this pain, depression, anxiety, sadness, and regret away from the forefront of my mind. I am trying to do things to distract, but the pain and feelings keep returning. I keep praying, reading the Bible, asking for calmness of the heart and mind, asking for a miracle. Lord, I need Your help. I'm afraid I'm not going to make it. I'm afraid there will be no end to this pain, anxiety, and overwhelming regret, sadness, and depression. God, please help me.

While laid up and hurting as I was, there is plenty of time to think and reflect. When my worry, pain, and panic were most severe—most excruciating—I was driven to depths of fear like never before. Not because it was the most painful, but because it was over a long period of time, and I was helpless, thinking it was permanent.

I read, I fought, I tried what I could. Nothing helped except turning to God again and asking for help. I prayed in tears, at night, all alone, revealed, naked before the Lord, stripped clean of my sense of control. I admitted that I was infinitesimal, not worthy of anything, but knew that God shows mercy and grace. That is when I realized that I thought I believed, but I had not really embraced my belief fully, my faith, my commitment to God, to Christ (the manifestation of God), and to the Spirit of God that is inside each of us.

Each night in my pain and panic, I read the Bible, devotions, and words of God on the internet. I sought God's power and love.

I kept repeating, like a mantra, Philippians 4:5-7: "The Lord is near. Do not be anxious about anything, but in everything, by prayer and petition, with thanksgiving, present your requests to God. And the peace of God, which transcends all understanding, will guard your hearts and your minds" (my heart and mind).

I believed that God would help me get through, survive another sleep-deprived night, another day of pain, panic, and anxiety. I would Google phrases like "God, please help me"; "God and mindfulness to help deal with pain, anxiety, and panic"; and "Jesus, help me with my pain."

I realized that I was on the fence—a convenient believer who had constructed a philosophy, a way to get through life. But it didn't work, at least during this time when all else was failing to help. I had to reach out to God with 100 percent of my heart, mind, and soul.

Each night, I fixed in my mind the image of Jesus reaching out, holding my hand, and saying, "Calm down. I'm with you." It was praying, at first for God, for Jesus, not to abandon me. Then I realized that my prayer should be for me not to abandon, not to deny, not to retreat from God, from Jesus.

Then on February 10, 2016, six weeks after this journey of pain and panic began, I stumbled upon a daily devotional by Pastor Rick Warren, in which he emphasized working at my problem from God's viewpoint—to see the bigger picture. He wrote about the apostle Paul being chained in prison for two years and how, during that time period, Paul wrote most of the New Testament, and how even some of Nero's family became believers.

I had been so very depressed for so long, and then I read Rick Warren's words. They reminded me of what I already knew but had let pain and worry block out. "There is a reason," I had been told many years earlier. But I had to search for it.

Why was God slowing me down? Why did He force me into a place of pain, panic, and anxiety that I felt was unbearable and never going to end? Now I know: God was giving me the opportunity to get closer to Him, to grow spiritually.

It has taken me a long time to understand and accept that all of us are given pain to endure, that suffering tests and educates our will and souls, and that it may seem unfair and unjust, especially when we are given more than the normal dose. But to let pain invade your mind and spirit, to torture your soul, to diminish your faith only makes it worse and gives it a negative power that it was not designed to have.

Through my most intense pain and recovery, I have learned to be more patient, accepting, and appreciative, especially of Diane; my children, grandchildren, family, and friends; and the life I have led thus far. I learned that I am not in control, although at times I keep trying to be. This has strengthened my relationship with God—my dependence on Him. God's presence has become stronger in me. I feel that I am in a continual dialogue with Him.

I also have learned to be more empathetic, understanding, and giving to others who are in pain—to pay attention, to not ignore, to reach out, to connect—even if it is only to say, "I understand what you are going through" or "I'm thinking about you" or "I'm wishing you the best" or "I'm saying a prayer for you" or "How are you doing? Are you feeling any better?" or thinking, "How can I help?"—and taking action. I will never "downplay" or "blow off" someone's physical or emotional pain again. I asked God to bring me health so that I can do better with the remainder of my life, contributing and helping others.

I have come to believe that there is a reason for pain to come into our lives: as a mechanism for development of ourselves and our souls—if we remain open to what can be learned—and if we don't allow bitterness and resentment to dominate.

I am not sure how to define God (I don't know if anyone really can with 100 percent certainty), but I do know that He exists, and I feel His presence. I do know that when I am separated from that presence (from God) because of ego, pain, resentment, or disappointment, I become disconnected from who I was designed to be.

Many years ago, shortly after Art Miller hired me to provide outplacement counseling to executives who had lost their jobs, I worked with an executive from Aetna (Mike Anstey), who said to me about being a soldier fighting during World War II, "This was not an experience I would have selected, but I would not give up what I learned from that experience for a million dollars." It took Mike a very long time to obtain a new job. He was sixty years old when he began and sixty-two (if I recall correctly) when his job-hunting journey ended. He felt the same about being fired and the long, painful job-hunting process and fear that he might never work again.

This is how I feel about the pain I have endured: I would not choose to have all this pain—any of this pain, especially this most recent pain. But I do believe I am a better person as a result and that I have moved closer to the way God designed me—closer to achieving the purpose of my life and my intended destiny.

For Reflection and Discussion

1. What pains, disappointments, and injustices have you let invade your mind and spirit, perhaps torturing your soul and diminishing your faith?

2. Have your pains, disappointments, and injustices helped you and your soul to grow, develop, and evolve to a better place, to achieve an inner peacefulness, and to become the person you have been designed to be? If not, what are you willing to do about it?

CHAPTER 41

Learn to Enjoy the Good Moments

It seems easy to get caught up in bad moments and let them take over our lives. Do you do that to yourself? Years ago, I read that we need to see and experience the bad to understand and appreciate the good; maybe that is so. Maybe we need both the good and bad to grow and develop—the yin and yang of life. Rick Warren, author of *The Purpose Driven Life,* is quoted as saying, "Transformation is a process, and as life happens there are tons of ups and downs. It's a journey of discovery—there are moments on mountaintops and moments in deep valleys of despair."

How do you feel about the bad moments? Do they hold you back from being who you were designed to be? Do you believe you can use the good moments to help overcome what bad moments can do to you and to the development of your soul?

Our first family vacation was to Cape Cod, Massachusetts; we stayed in a rented house about one mile from the beach. We crawled over the Bourne Bridge, turning our three-hour drive closer to five hours. The kids grew antsy when we stalled in the bridge traffic. Tensions rose, exacerbated I'm sure by my own words, behavior, and restlessness. Kevin was almost age five and Katie, four months past her second birthday.

Once we settled into the three-bedroom ranch-style house, we walked the short distance to Lewis Bay, unleashing Kevin to run barefoot through the wet sand, with Katie trying to keep up. The sun was setting. Diane and I held hands as we strolled. All the tensions from the drive and life evaporated—a good moment.

The next day was reserved for the beach. I was probably even more excited than the kids. I grew up on Long Island near the beaches and, at a young age, learned to ride waves—body surfing. The bigger the wave, the better. It had been almost fifteen years since my last wave-riding days on the Atlantic and Far Rockaway beaches, wading and swimming into the ocean, diving over and under the waves, and positioning myself for that *moment*. I had this uncanny intuitive feel for the correct spot and wave and was rarely disappointed, often riding all the way to the shore. I rarely missed.

I felt like a kid that first morning as my anticipation grew, but equally important was my desire to teach Kevin the art of riding waves. He was young, but not much younger than me, I thought, when I bolted from my mother and ran into the ocean, swam until my head was barely above the water, stood on the tips of my toes, and caught my first wave. It was a feeling and memory that will be with me forever—a good moment.

Sea Gull Beach was big, sandy, exciting, and beautiful.

Kevin, it turned out, was a bit too young to ride the waves I envisioned him catching, making me think that I was probably much older than I remembered when I rode my first wave.

He was hesitant to go out as far into the ocean as I had wanted, but he overcame his fear and joined me. I held his hand securely, as wave upon wave tried to knock him down. When we got too deep for him to stand, I lifted him to my shoulder, wrapping my arms around his body, shielding him as best I could, while he tightly clutched my neck and burrowed his head into the safety of my body—another good moment.

When Kevin wasn't with me in the water, I body surfed, wave upon wave. If there had been a beach competition for who caught the most waves and who rode them the farthest, I surely would have won.

Sand dunes were all along the back of the beach, and when Kevin and Katie were not in the water or playing in the sand—digging, splashing, and building—they loved climbing up, down, and through the sand dunes.

Kevin always seemed to find a stick of some sort and use it as his imagination fed his play. Katie always seemed to find something interesting to show us. At the end of each day, we were like pack mules, riding our bikes back to the rented home on Lorena Road.

One evening, after grilling hamburgers and hot dogs, just as we were about to eat, we saw a skunk whose head was stuck inside an empty box of popcorn. He was stumbling around in circles—shaking his head, left and right, and up and down, trying to get that box off his nose and mouth.

Diane and I thought it was funny; the kids thought it was hilarious. We laughed but simultaneously felt bad for the skunk because we soon realized that he was not able to free himself from the popcorn box. I thought of going outside and helping him. In my mind, I'd sneak up on the distressed skunk, and when he stopped to catch his breath, pull off the popcorn box and then run as fast as I could to safety. Diane convinced me otherwise, telling me that I would have to sleep under the sky if I got sprayed by the skunk. Instead, I called the police, who eventually sent Animal Control to the rescue. It was one of those unique experiences and bonding moments.

Each morning, I would bike up South Sea to a deli and buy the local newspaper and occasionally bagels for breakfast. In the evening, we played games with the kids, played miniature golf, rode the bikes, or strolled to the bay. Before dinner, Kevin and I would throw the Frisbee to each other or play catch with the tennis ball, using the baseball gloves we had brought. One day, we rode our bikes along the rail trail and, on another, we drove out to the National Sea Shore.

This first vacation was all we had wanted it to be. There were no cell phones or texting back then. The problems of the world and worries we left behind didn't go away, but they got buried so deeply underneath the joy of vacation that our peaceful karma was not disturbed.

One morning, before we headed to the beach, Diane called her mother, who had gone in for a medical test. Not a big deal, we were told. When Diane hung up the telephone, she was ashen. Her mother had cancer, she was told, and needed laryngectomy surgery. The cancer was brought on by cigarette smoking.

A laryngectomy involves removing the voice box; separating the airway from the mouth, nose, and esophagus; cutting a hole in the front of the neck, pulling the trachea forward, and attaching it so the person can breathe through the hole in the neck (stoma) instead of through the mouth and nose.

I admired Diane's mother. Pound for pound, she was the strongest person I have ever met. She was a tough, stubborn Irish woman who never encountered an obstacle, challenge, or job she felt she couldn't handle. She was not quite five feet tall and barely weighed ninety-five pounds, if that.

To give you an understanding of what I mean by strong, when a tree died in her yard, her son-in-law (my brother-in-law), Glenn, told her that he would come during the weekend to cut down the dead tree, using his chain saw. But she was not one to wait, and before the weekend arrived, using a hand-held bow saw, this tiny woman in her seventies not only cut the tree down by herself but also cut the trunk and branches into pieces that could be carted away easily.

She was not the kind of person you would want to tangle with; this I learned early in my marriage. But if you were in a fox hole, as the saying goes, she is the one you would want in there with you.

Diane's mother had the surgery and lost her voice. She loved engaging in conversation, and now it was difficult, mainly because many people (including me, I am sad to admit) had great trouble understanding her. She refused to use any kind of mechanical device to aid her.

When it came to eating, she had to chew her food slowly into the tiniest of pieces so it wouldn't get stuck in her throat. Eventually she had to puree all her food. Her weight dropped dangerously low. But none of this prevented her from cooking large family dinners, when all four of her children with husbands and seven grandkids congregated at her house.

When it snowed, she shoveled in such a way that you doubted that snow ever fell in her driveway, or on her walkway, or on the sidewalk in front of her home.

Using clippers—manual, of course—she trimmed her hedges to perfection, climbing up a rickety wooden ladder. Her lawn, flowers, and bushes all stood out for their neatness.

She survived and prevailed for an additional twenty-one years. At her funeral, Diane, in her eulogy, said, "God was waiting for her to arrive in heaven to straighten out the angels." That's how tough she was.

After the call about the surgery and our initial shock, when everyone else went to bed, I thought about how transitory life can be. At one moment, all can seem so peaceful, wonderful, and joyful, and then in the next moment, the hammer falls.

As I write this, I think of my older brother, Gene, who woke up one day, at age forty-six, to discover that he had multiple myeloma and how his life changed drastically. He was told that he had only a few years to live.

Gene is still living, having survived now for almost twenty-five years since the diagnosis. During his battle, his wife and best friend of many years died, rather suddenly, of another form of cancer.

Gene has a metal rod in his leg and lives with continual discomfort. Most of his physical pain is subdued by various medications. He has four wonderful children who have given him nine grandkids. Family means everything to Gene, and despite his discomfort, pain, and physical limitations, he accomplishes much of what is important to him.

He is often on the road, from Spokane to Nashville to Virginia, visiting his kids and grandkids and creating those special moments that make his life rich. The way Gene continues to live his life, given his physical limitations, is an inspiration to me, as are his attitude and determination—the older brother still teaches the younger one.

One day, while I was waiting for a client to show up for a dinner meeting, I telephoned Gene using my cell phone. He told me he needed to have a bone marrow transplant. He had undergone various kinds of treatments and surgeries over the previous nine years, but now the cancer had returned with a vengeance. The physicians found new lesions in the bones of his legs and spine. To prepare him for the transplant, his body needed to be radiated and then given high doses of chemotherapy over a three-month period. All were designed to destroy the cancer cells, but in the process, they would also destroy his entire immune system.

I told my client about the call. If I hadn't, he might not understand why I was not very attentive. My client then told me how he was in Switzerland with his wife sipping wine, looking out at the Alps, thinking how wonderful life was, and how he came to believe that things have a way of balancing out. He put it in mathematical terms and explained to me the statistical phenomenon of Regression to the Mean.

He then went on to say how, shortly after that vacation, his son grew extremely ill. After one hospital couldn't find the cure, his son was transferred to another hospital. And after an extended stay at the second hospital, he was placed in hospice—a few days from death. My client said that the treatments that were tried over many months failed. He and his wife took turns staying in the hospital room with their son—eight-hour shifts, twenty-four hours a day, seven days a week. He lost his job while he cared for his son.

He told me how each day he did research to see if there was a cure—something else to try that would provide some ray of hope. He identified a new drug that had not been approved by the FDA but was legal in a European country. He got referred to a high-level FDA official to whom he explained the situation and pleaded with him to allow his son's doctors to try the medication. The FDA granted an exception. He contacted the president of the European company, seeking the drug. The drug was flown overnight and administered to his son. It cured him—it was a miracle.

I have come to recognize that we have all been given glorious moments to enjoy and revel in—to forever remember—that lift us up, if we let them. And they can come at any time and in many different forms. Sometimes they are big and dramatic, like a saved life, but often they are small and quite simple, like holding hands, or strolling with friends, or a blue sky on a sunny day, or a grandchild's smile.

It has taken much time and reflection for me to recognize the power of those moments, particularly the small ones—to feel them in such a way that they become forever part of me. And I have come to understand that they can serve as a buffer and balance against those other moments that we are all given, the ones that can destroy us if we let them.

For Reflection and Discussion

1. Have you learned to appreciate the good moments in your life? If not, why not?
2. Do you use the good moments to help balance the bad moments? If not, why not?

CHAPTER 42

Love Can Prevail

If you have raised a difficult child, you know how frustrating it can be. If you haven't, you might say, "What's the big deal?" or you may empathetically imagine the emotional pain of being pulled into a vortex through love and commitment. If you have a difficult sibling, parent, spouse, or loved one, you know the pain. The same is true if you are the one being thought of as "the difficult one." I know. The die is cast, the hand dealt. You do the best you are capable of doing. Whatever the outcome, it becomes an opportunity to develop your soul and come closer to achieving the purpose of your life and your intended destiny.

"Give me the pearl-handled ones," the gray-haired doctor calmly said to the nurse. Without hesitation, she quickly left the room and returned carrying forceps—all before the next push. It was all happening so fast. Hands were inserted into the birth canal, aligning the pearl-handled forceps. And then the doctor stood up and pulled. His muscles strained as he pulled...and pulled...and pulled. I was in a daze, unsure what to think or do. Out popped our child. Welcome to the world, dear son.

He was being born with the umbilical cord around his neck, causing his heart rate to drop by half. I was aware but numbed by what was happening and could happen, and the suddenness of it all. This can't be—can't be the culmination of nine months of excitement and anticipation!

The calm, quiet, low-lighted Leboyer birth process we wanted so badly was not to be. The warm water we had prepared in which to gently float and bathe our newborn son was replaced by lights to treat his jaundiced skin. His beautiful, tiny, round face was reshaped and bruised by the use of forceps.

"Not to worry," we were told. "He will be fine. The heartbeat is strong. The face and head will heal and return to normalcy. The lights will treat his jaundiced skin." We were relieved.

Our bonding moment lasted only a few seconds before our baby was whisked away. We had to wait almost one week before we could bring him home.

His first week of life was spent in a hospital, under lights and the careful eyes of nurses and doctors. He was fed by bottle, not the breast; and when we were finally able to bring him home, we couldn't get him to feed by breast, no matter how patiently Diane tried. We exhausted all the advice and techniques that well-meaning experts had given us.

We were disappointed; we had wanted it all to go perfectly. "It's not such a big deal," we said to each other. "He is healthy and happy, and that's all that matters."

With Dr. Spock's book in hand, we were ready, if not ill-prepared, for the role of parents. Diane was the oldest of four and had a lot of experience helping raise her younger siblings. I, on the other hand, was the youngest of four and had not raised anything living.

We doted, loved, hugged, kissed, and laughed our way through the early years.

Periodically I would think that parenting for the first time was like being in a dark room, surrounded by the kind of darkness you would find in a cave. I thought of Howes Caverns and the tour guide who turns the lights out and asks if you can see your hands before your eyes, and you can't. In my thoughts and analogy of that kind of darkened room, you can feel doorknobs, and each door represents a decision you make as a young parent. You open the door and see what is on the other side. You want the best; you want to make the right decisions, but there is little experience to guide you.

There are others you can ask, who have traveled similar roads, and there was always Dr. Spock's books. But truth be told, we were on our own with this tiny baby we loved more than anything in the world. And we wanted to do everything the right way. We wanted every reaction to what we did to be perfect. But it wasn't always as we wanted. I fretted and worried and second-guessed. That is what I do; it is my nature. I can't help myself. This has led to many sleep-deprived nights filled with ponderings and ruminations.

Then one day, we realized that something was wrong, camouflaged by everyday contact, so we didn't see the progression. One day we woke up and admitted, "We are over our heads, out of our league, beyond our capability." And as our eyes opened to the reality of the situation, we said, "How could we not have seen this?" We went to professional after professional seeking advice and solutions. And we tried things. And tried and tried—and we never stopped loving, believing, trying, and praying.

After many years, a corner was turned, and progress was made.

From the abyss emerged a changed person—tears of joy following years of torturous worry, frustration, and anger. We celebrated a second birth.

When that moment came, for reasons unknown, late at night, all alone, I decided to pick up the Bible I had read many years earlier. I closed my eyes, opened it up to a page, and pointed my finger, thinking, hoping that some answer would be provided. Here were the words I pointed to and read: "We have to celebrate and rejoice. This brother of yours was dead, and has come back to life. He was lost and is found" (Luke 15:11).

Shortly after that, I received the following letter from my changed son:

> I realize that I am very lucky to have a father who is as devoted, patient, empathetic, and generous as you. I have no excuses, justifications, or even any real explanations for my hesitance to regain direction in my life. I believe I am now starting to gain momentum again and will continue to take action and progress into a new phase of my life. It's like life is the ocean, and we are just floating around in the surf. Sometimes a wave comes, and we let it pass or duck under it, and sometimes we paddle as hard as we can to meet it, and we take it for a ride. There are also waves that crash into us whether we like it or not, the ones that pull us down, twist us around, only letting go when it seems we couldn't possibly hold our breath any longer. When I was little, we were at the beach trying to ride waves together, and the waves were big. You held me with your arms, and I felt the water around me, pulling me in all directions. I knew that you were strong, and I knew that you were not going to let go of me. I just want to say thank you for everything.

My son may not have learned how to ride waves that day in the ocean, but he learned something far more important. He recalled a moment he will forever remember, that touched him in a way I didn't know or appreciate at the time. I will forever cherish this note he sent to me, as well as the changes that followed in him and in me, over a long period of time. They were not unlike the changes that occurred in my father and me as we allowed our relationship to heal.

Difficulties between loved ones can lead to something else—a rebirth of sorts—if you and they put in the labor, give it time, and seek God's assistance. It doesn't always happen, but it can.

I have come to understand and recognize that my son is much more like me than I thought, and perhaps I have become more like my father than I realized—a connection that flows through the generations. Life goes on. Love can prevail. It is part of who we are.

For Reflection and Discussion

1. How well have you dealt with a difficult child, family member, or loved one? What impact has this had on the development of you and your soul?

CHAPTER 43

Letting Go and Moving On

Do you need to let go of something in your life that is holding you and the development of your soul back?

It was late at night. The house was dark, except for one light where I sat. I was trying to write, but a mosquito was drawn to me. I swiped and missed. I swiped again and slammed my hands together, hoping to crush him—again and again. I could no longer see him, but I sensed him and felt him. I swiped, slapped, and slammed again and again.

I didn't know if he was real or imaginary. I couldn't see the dead mosquito body. But he was in my head—I sensed him, felt him—so I kept swiping, slapping, and slamming. I must have looked ridiculous, bobbing and weaving and swiping at air.

I thought, "Isn't this reflective of life and what we can do to ourselves?" We can get something into our heads that bugs us and distracts us, and we can't let go of it. It stays in our heads, controlling us and preventing us from focusing and accomplishing more, or sending us down a path we may end up regretting.

Then I realized that it was time to get up, shut off the light in the room, shut the door, and move to a new place where there were no imaginary, or real, mosquitoes to bug and distract me.

For Reflection and Discussion
1. What doors in your mind and life do you need to close, and what new doors do you need to open?
2. How will you achieve this, and who will help you?

SECTION 5

Don't Give Up—The Journey Continues

CHAPTER 44

Don't Waste the Opportunity God Has Given to You

In *Reflections on the Art of Living*, Joseph Campbell writes, "Opportunities to find deeper powers within ourselves come when life seems most challenging." How do you view and treat the difficulties of life? How about when they are major and feel overwhelming? Do they tarnish or strengthen your determination and soul?

I was driving home in a blizzard from a meeting in New York City, on the winding Merritt Parkway. It was February, and the snowflakes were large and swirling, blowing at me in dense, unrelenting waves—the kind of snow that totally blinds, where you can't see in front of you, can't see the road, and can't see where you are headed. No other cars were around, no taillights to follow. My senses became heightened. I became acutely aware that I could easily head in the wrong direction, off the road, and crash, that something could suddenly emerge that could throw me off path, or that I could, in my blindness, steer the car into a ditch, into a tree, into a snow bank. Not unlike life.

As I drove in fear that evening, I drew upon a story my father loved telling about driving across the country and coming to a road that took him over the mountains into California. As the story goes, it was a narrow, winding road with no guardrails. He was driving inches from the edge, where one false move could send him crashing into the valley below. As he ascended the mountain, the drive and drop from the road grew increasingly ominous. He spoke of doubting and wanting to turn back. Then he saw a sign beside the road: "Thousands have driven this road, so can you."

To me, that story has always been about not being afraid to try, despite a lack of experience, knowledge, concern, fear, self-doubt, handicaps, obstacles, or whatever holds one back.

It was a story that was in my mind shortly after starting at People Management, inexperienced and unprepared, really just an immature and unaware kid. I was only a few days into working as a part-time counselor, teaching job hunting to people who had lost their jobs, when Arthur F. Miller Jr., the owner and founder, asked me, "How would you like to do a search?"

"What's a search?"

"We have an assignment from Bostich to help them hire a director of manufacturing engineering. Here's a transcript of the interview I had with the hiring manager and a directory listing manufacturing engineers at companies. Read the transcript, and call me with questions."

"OK," was my response.

I read the transcript but had little idea of what the job actually entailed. I had no idea how to go about conducting this retained search assignment. This was manufacturing and engineering, worlds I had no experience in. I called Art, but he was nowhere to be found—not that he didn't care or wouldn't have been responsive to my questions if I could have tracked him down.

Art, by nature, is a combination of Johnny Appleseed and Don Quixote. He is a pioneer who moves about on frontiers, dropping seeds and moving on, leaving the tending to someone else, and there is a side to him that believes in pursuing the seemingly impossible.

He hired people and gave them the opportunity to grow but was rarely around. I was one of those hires, one of the seemingly impossible, a seed trying to take root and grow, a seed with few developed skills and little business knowledge, a seed with a host of confidence issues, but with God-given potential—as we all have.

I figured out how to do the search. I drove the road before me with my father's words as my passenger.

Later that year, Art asked if I would like to do another search for a company called Vitramon. They made ceramic capacitors. They wanted to hire a technical leader. I had no science background (never took courses in biology, chemistry, or physics). What little engineering and manufacturing I understood came from completing the assignment for Bostich and a few MAP counseling sessions. I was fearful and unsure but agreed to work with Art. He said, "We'll meet together at the company, and we'll do the interview together to learn about the job together. I'll be there to help you with this assignment." I had just turned twenty-seven years old.

I showed up at 8:30 a.m. on the designated day to meet with Vitramon's president. I was early and waited for Art to arrive. The president's secretary called me to her desk and handed me her telephone. It was Art on the other end of the line. "I can't make it—you'll have to do the interview alone."

I wanted to run, to hide, to escape this obligation I was so ill-prepared to assume. I thought of the story my father had told me and walked through the door to the president's office, conducted the interview, and completed the assignment.

Many years later, I was conducting a search for a foreign company that was seeking a new general manager for its American business. I recognized the name of the candidate who was before me. He was an entrepreneur who had built and sold a company he had started, earning him more than $25 million, if I recall correctly. "Why is he interested in this job?" I wondered. He told me how he invested all his money in internet stocks, and then the stock market crashed, and the companies he invested in folded. He was broke and needed a job.

The roads we are given to drive can become daunting. They can challenge the spirit, test our core.

I have interviewed many successful people who started out in life with little or nothing; living in poverty; no parents or other family to speak of; educational deficiency; racism; bullying; language barriers; a physical disability; living in a ghetto; drug addiction or being under the thumb of a totalitarian regime and then escaping and coming to America, not knowing the language, not knowing anyone. If you have met such people, their stories are inspiring. They used the obstacles, difficulties, and handicaps they experienced to fortify their strength and determination. They had fear but were fearless in how they went about trying.

We are all victims in some way, but it is important not to develop a victim mentality.

I have interviewed people who were born into wealth, with high expectations placed on them, and incredible support. They, too, were victims—of expectation, comfort, and perhaps a sense of entitlement, unintentionally fostered by those who loved them most. Some became highly successful, recognizing that they were victims of their privileged circumstances, and used being a "victim" to fortify their strength and determination, to break free from their bonds, just as those who were born with little have used their circumstances. We are all victims—no one escapes.

I have interviewed people who have lost their jobs; lost their homes; lost their family; forced to live on the street who have climbed back up; people who were falsely accused; sent to prison; sent to war; lost a child to an early death; lost a wife, a brother, a sister, a friend; were the subject of intense neglect, bullying, torture, and torment; people with life-threatening injuries; life-threatening illnesses; incredible tragedy to deal with; devastating pain to persevere through; an addiction to overcome; losing what they had; facing no job prospects, no future, no hope.

A forge heats steel so that it can be shaped and formed, only to be suddenly thrust out of the comforts of the heat into coolness so it can become what it is destined to become. It is the same with people. And just as a diamond needs pressure to be formed into its splendor, it is the same with people.

Everyone has issues to overcome. Life spares no one.

Since my youth, I have carried with me the poem "If" by Rudyard Kipling, given to me by my father, in his attempt to open my eyes.

> If you can keep your head when all about you
> Are losing theirs and blaming it on you,
> If you can trust yourself when all men doubt you,
> But make allowance for their doubting too;
> If you can wait and not be tired by waiting,
> Or being lied about, don't deal in lies,
> Or being hated, don't give way to hating,
> And yet don't look too good, nor talk too wise;
>
> If you can dream—and not make dreams your master;
> If you can think—and not make thoughts your aim;
> If you can meet with Triumph and Disaster
> And treat those two imposters just the same;
> If you can bear to hear the truth you've spoken
> Twisted by knaves to make a trap for fools,
> Or, watch the things you gave your life to, broken,
> And stoop and build 'em up with worn-out tools;

If you can make one heap of all your winnings
And risk it on one turn of pitch-and-toss,
And lose, and start again at your beginnings
And never breathe a word about your loss;
If you can force your heart and nerve and sinew
To serve your turn long after they are gone,
And so hold on when there is nothing in you
Except the will which says to them: "Hold on!"

If you can talk with crowds and keep your virtue,
Or walk with Kings—nor lose your common touch,
If neither foes nor loving friends can hurt you,
If all men count with you, but none too much;
If you can fill the unforgiving minute
With sixty seconds' worth of distance run,
Yours is the Earth and everything that's in it,
And—which is more—you'll be a Man, my son!

In contrast, I have met people, whether born with little, a lot, or somewhere in between, who use their circumstances, obstacles, and handicaps as an excuse. They live their lives with a victim mentality. The road is too daunting, the path too hard—unaware or denying what they do to themselves; their fight, determination, and discipline diminished or gone.

There is no doubt that life shapes us. But we can shape the way our lives unfold by how we respond to those blizzards and daunting roads—with all their hazards.

As I have gotten older, I have come to realize that there is even more to my father's story. I have come to understand how it is much easier to remain in my nest, to stay in my comfort zone into which I can settle, but from which I need a hand, occasionally, to challenge me, to push me, to encourage me to evolve. To ignore those hands, those people, that spirit, to pass on those opportunities, to flee from those moments is to close my eyes and begin the process of burying what God has given me.

For Reflection and Discussion

1. Do you have a victim mentality? Have you allowed life circumstances, obstacles, difficulties, and handicaps to tarnish your soul and spirit and hold you back? Are you wasting the opportunity God has given to you? If yes, what has gotten in your way?

2. Despite circumstances, obstacles, difficulties, and handicaps, how have you responded to shape the way your life has unfolded in a positive way? What else can you do?

3. Who challenges, pushes, and encourages you to continue evolving, to more fully use the giftedness and opportunity God has given you?

CHAPTER 45

Don't Miss the Bus

Life is full of distractions that can cause you to lose your way—temporarily, maybe permanently (hopefully not.) Have you experienced this? Are you experiencing this? In the beginning of this book, "The Importance of Home," I wrote about the importance of having homes that anchor, ground, and connect us to something positive to give our lives focus, clarity, meaning, and purpose. Do you have such *homes*? If so, do you use them to become a better person, the person God designed you to be?

I had a wild dream that combined all sorts of people in all sorts of situations they shouldn't be in with me: on a boat, in the water; running down a street; the character Sawyer from the TV show *Lost* cutting my hair, but it was not being cut; a girl I had a crush on in high school enticing me; being in a political group; being in a tour group; being alone; looking for my jacket, opening the closet door to find a round coat rack, spinning the rack and the jackets falling to the floor, desperately looking for mine; and being aware that I had to catch a bus that was about to leave, realizing I had no pants on, and running to catch the bus, barefoot, down streets, through alleys.

In the dream, I kept getting distracted, losing my way, climbing steps, entering rooms, being in places from movies and TV shows, from my past, feeling compelled, looking, seeing, experiencing (it felt so real as dreams can sometimes seem), but not wanting to miss the bus, which I was going to miss if I couldn't get control of myself—couldn't get there on time.

I woke up thinking, "My dreams are rarely this wild. What's going on? What's the dream saying to me?" I tried to recall what bits and parts I could, tried to put it together, to make sense of it. I was groggy and fell back to sleep.

Two days later, I was fast asleep and began coughing in such a way that I felt my insides were about to come out. I picked up my pillow and blanket and left the bedroom to sleep on the couch. I didn't want to disturb Diane. Back to sleep. I coughed again, even more loudly, more violently. I felt that the house could shake from my coughing. I got up, drank a cup of water, took cough medicine, and sucked on a throat lozenge, but each time I lay down and put my head on the pillow, I began to cough violently. "Something is trying to come out," I thought. "What is it?"

I let thoughts and feelings float in and out of my mind. I got a pen and pad and said to myself, "Something is coming." I began thinking of people I have met, whom I have interviewed, who let me into their lives, whom I admire—not just for their professional successes, but for how they live their lives, how they give of themselves to others despite distractions, temptations, difficulties, obstacles, time pressures, personal challenges, and tensions, and for how they allow God to be a part of their lives. They seem to know what is important, and their lives reflect that awareness. I also thought of people who don't seem to care about others and their souls, and then about those whom I met who struggled with doing what is right. For a brief moment, I thought, "That's me, what I have been saddled with."

Then my mind suddenly drifted to a conversation I had the day before with Ralph Mattson, a long-ago mentor who told me about working with troubled youth. He coached them to success. They listened to him, he said. They followed his structure, his recommendations. They changed. Success was achieved.

People who like to coach, who hang in there by your side, are wonderfully needed and important. I'm more your splash and dash type. I like advising, influencing, quickly helping, making a positive splash, but then moving on. I just don't have the needed patience. I don't like having the ongoing obligation.

I asked Ralph, "What if the person doesn't want to be helped?"

"There isn't much you can do," he said.

Then I started thinking about my life and how much I had changed since meeting Diane. I thought of the battles I've had, not just with her, but more with myself. How easy it has been at times for me to lose sight of where I want to go, what kind of person I want to be and am designed to be, and how much farther I needed to travel.

Finally, I thought of God and how He came into my life, but I had to be receptive. Just because I became a believer doesn't mean the path became easy. There are a lot of distractions, I realized, that can cause me to miss the bus.

For Reflection and Discussion

1. What stands in your way of becoming a better person, the kind of person you would like to be, the person you have been designed to be?

CHAPTER 46

What I Believe

I believe that God has designed each of us and that the purpose of the lives we have been given is to keep evolving ourselves and our souls toward that design. This perspective has been enormously beneficial to me, bringing me clarity of purpose, a more meaningful life, and a way to measure success.

Pastor T. D. Jakes writes in his book on destiny that "It is not only a destination, a goal, a dream, a purpose; it is an inner process of becoming all you were meant to be."

I believe our design is composed of four broad components, which I refer to as "keys":

1. **Our giftedness—our natural talent.** I believe God possesses all possible gifts and talents, that He puts a unique combination of them inside each of us, and that part of the purpose of our lives and intended destinies is to apply these God-given gifts and talents and appropriately manage them.
2. **Our desire to seek a relationship with God.** If we don't allow God into our lives; and if we don't allow His presence to grow within us, I believe a major part of our design—the way God created us—is not being expressed or developed.
3. **A giving, caring, compassionate, and loving way of interacting with people and the world.** It is the way we express the natural goodness God put inside each of us, and when we fulfill this key aspect of our design, our lives have more meaning and purpose.
4. **A drive to learn, grow, and develop through difficulties, obstacles, hardships, and challenges.** I believe this fourth key aspect of our design is a major way God shapes us.

I believe that only by evolving our souls toward these four key aspects of our design can we achieve our intended destinies and life purpose. If we don't use our giftedness well; let God into our lives; show grace, kindness, compassion, and love; and accept and appreciate that God helps each of us evolve our souls through difficulties, obstacles, hardships, and challenges, along with positive experiences, then we are not doing all we can do to realize the purpose of our lives and our intended destinies.

I believe the purpose of our lives is to develop as best we can, to become as God has designed us—in His image.

For Reflection and Discussion

   1.   What do you believe is the purpose of your life?

CHAPTER 47

An Admission

As I bring this book to an end, I want to reveal something important about myself that I have not yet said but you may not be surprised to learn. For a long time, I wished I was different than who I am. There were many things about me I didn't like and much I saw in others that I envied. But no one knew this about me—I hid it well.

This feeling didn't change for a long time, and it still lingers, periodically rearing its ugly head. It did begin to change, but not until I did the following:

- I started using my giftedness—my natural talent as identified by the Motivated Abilities Pattern (MAP)—in a positive manner and effectively managed my nature, which has been challenging and freeing. I stopped wishing and trying to be who I was not meant to be.
- I recognized that I was uniquely gifted by God—as we all are—and that I have a tremendous mechanism to experience meaning and purpose built in through my giftedness—as we all do.
- I accepted God and His unconditional love, realized that He speaks to us through life experiences, often punctuating by sending people into our lives, and began listening for His messages and trying to understand them.
- I allowed the natural goodness that is inside me—inside each of us —to become strengthened through use, which we all can do, working hard at emptying my heart of disappointment, resentment, envy, anger, and nothingness, and filling it, as much as I can, with understanding, acceptance, and giving. I tried to fill the glass of me, my soul, as much as I can, with the good instead of the bad. Doing

so has helped give my life even more meaning and purpose and brought me even more peace of mind and spirit.

- I accepted that obstacles, challenges, and difficulties that are meant to develop and strengthen our cores—our souls—and prayed for God to grant me peace of mind and spirit that comes with faith and acceptance.

- I came to understand that the purpose of my life is not a single event or a moment, or an activity or a role, but to live, learn, and evolve toward how God has designed me. And what is true for me, I believe, is true for you.

Sometimes you have to leave where you are to open doors to what you can become—how you were designed to be. My journey continues.

Acknowledgments

Writing this book has been a long process, beginning in 2002, with huge gaps of time in between. By 2008, I decided to share what I had written with some people and sought their reactions and suggestions. This was encouraging but also eye opening. I wish to acknowledge their assistance and thank them for being gracious with their time and for providing valuable perspective.

First, I am much appreciative of the sixteen people whose endorsements appear in the beginning of the book. Some didn't shy away at all in their suggestions. Others who read versions of the book and provided feedback include Marci Alborghetti, Bill Banis, Cheryl Buford, Cherie Calbon, Father John Calbon, Gene Darter (my brother), Eric Fellman, Jim Ferguson, Sister Marylouise Fennell, Mike Ferris, Mike Fisch, Pastor Bob Gattorna, Scott Gilyard, Audrey Goodman, Jeff Jernigan, Don Kiehl, Arthur F. Miller III, Joshua Miller, Kim Miller, Marty Petty, Ed Poff, Ken Ross, Rob Stevenson, Robert Waller, and Rick Wellock.

A special thank you goes to my former assistant Diane Cables and later, Libbye Morrris (my editor) who both worked tirelessly on correcting my grammatical errors, which I must admit were many. A special thank you also goes to Bruce Nygren, a senior editor at Waterbrook Multnomah, Random House, who donated his time and expertise, early in the process, to help me better focus and structure the book. His words of encouragement about the quality of my writing helped me overcome self-doubts that persisted throughout this project.

Then there is my wife, Diane, who puts up with me in many ways, for which I am forever grateful. Her love and candor are both a warm embrace and a protective shield.

ABOUT THE AUTHOR

Steven M. Darter

Steven Darter has a distinguished career as a consultant, author, educator, and speaker. For more than forty years, he has counseled people ranging from troubled teenagers to CEOs of Fortune 500 corporations on work, career, and life issues. He is the author of two books: *Lessons from Life: Four Keys to Living with More Meaning, Purpose, and Success (2018)*; and *Managing Yourself, Managing Others: Learn How to Improve Effectiveness, Productivity, and Work Satisfaction*, which has three editions (2001, 2011, and 2015).

During his long career, Steve has interviewed close to five thousand people. In each interview, he used SIMA® (The System for Motivated Abilities®) to understand the person's unique motivational design {Motivated Abilities Pattern® (MAP®)} and best paths for success; and in some cases, what had gotten in their way. This vantage point gave Steve an unusually close-up view of how peoples' lives unfolded, including their successes and failures, and the impact of decisions they made, actions they took, beliefs they adopted, course corrections they made, regrets, feelings of disappointment and failure, and satisfaction. He is a recognized expert in helping people understand the implications of SIMA and MAPs, and is known for his dynamic and engaging presentations, workshops, seminars, and team-building sessions.

In 1976, Steve started his consulting career with People Management Inc. (now SIMA International). In 1984, he was appointed Senior Vice President and Head of Executive Search and Selection; from 1990 to 2005, he was president of People Management Northeast Inc.; and from 1996 to 1999, he simultaneously served as chairman of the People Management partnership organization. In 2005, he formed People Management SMD, LLC.

Steve's consulting has focused on helping organizations improve results through a better understanding and positioning of people and helping people make good decisions about their life and work. He specializes in executive and management development, team development, selection, succession, and consultation on issues related to job fit, performance, and the effective utilization and management of strengths.

Steve has taught a career-counseling course to graduate counseling students at Saint Joseph College and an advanced practicum on "Managing to Strengths" to MBA students at the University of Hartford. His honors include being profiled as one of North America's top executive recruiters in the book *The New Career Makers*, based on survey results of CEOs, senior HR executives, and other business leaders.

He has an MS degree in education and an EdS degree in counseling from the State University of New York at Albany. His BS degree is in sociology from SUNY at Oswego.

The 2015 edition of Steve Darter's first book, **Managing Yourself, Managing Others: Learn How to Improve Effectiveness, Productivity, and Work Satisfaction**, is available through Amazon for paperback and Kindle, Smashwords for other ebook devices, and through all local bookstores.

For more information on Steve or to contact him:

www.StevenDarter.com

www.PeopleManagementSMD.com

Made in the USA
Columbia, SC
29 April 2018